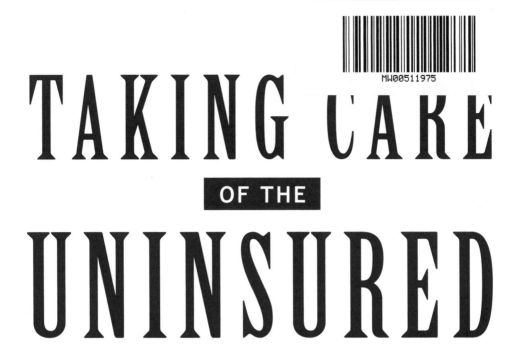

TAKING CARE
OF THE
UNINSURED

A Path to Reform

WAYNE STATE
UNIVERSITY

Taking Care of the Uninsured
A Path to Reform

by

James D. Chesney, PhD
Policy Initiatives Consulting Group
Ann Arbor, Michigan

Herbert C. Smitherman, Jr., MD, MPH, FACP
Assistant Dean, Community and Urban Health
Assistant Professor, Department of Medicine
and Karmanos Cancer Institute,
Wayne State University School of Medicine/Detroit Medical Center
President and CEO, Health Centers Detroit Foundation, Inc.
Detroit, Michigan

Cynthia Taueg, BSN, MPH, DHA
Vice President for Community Health
St. John Health
Warren, Michigan

Jennifer Mach, MD, MPH
Epidemiology and Biostatistics
Voices of Detroit Initiative (VODI)
Detroit, Michigan

Lucille Smith, MEd
Executive Director
Voices of Detroit Initiative (VODI)
Detroit, Michigan

WAYNE STATE
UNIVERSITY

Published by Wayne State University

The views and opinions expressed herein do not necessarily reflect those of Wayne State University or its Board of Governors.

ISBN 978-0-615-16276-8

Distributed by Partners Book Distributing
Holt, Michigan

Book Designed and Typeset by
Eastword Publications Development
Cleveland, Ohio

Voices of Detroit Initiative (VODI)
University Health Center (UHC) - 9D
4201 St. Antoine Blvd.
Detroit, Michigan 48201

This book is dedicated to the loving memory of

Dr. John B. Waller, Jr.,

who for more than a half century dedicated his life and
career to influencing, directing, and shaping local and
national public health policy for those without a voice.

Foreword

Taking Care of the Uninsured: A Path to Reform

Almost 50 million Americans are without health insurance and that number is increasing. This trend is mirrored in Detroit and Michigan, both of which have been weathering a severe economic decline in recent years. Of Detroit's nearly one million residents, 33 percent are covered by Medicaid and 20 percent have no health insurance at all.

Nationally, a lack of consensus on the way to proceed toward resolution promises that this crisis will only worsen in the foreseeable future. Faced by that certainty, safety net providers such as major academic health centers, which disproportionately provide care to the underserved and uninsured in our cities, can no longer afford to wait for national leadership to act.

Wayne State University, of which I am president, is a research institution of worldwide reputation with a major school of medicine and vigorous partnerships with teaching hospitals and health centers. Our School of Medicine has served the citizens of Detroit and Michigan for nearly 140 years; with nearly 2,500 medical students and trainees and 2,250 full-time and volunteer faculty members, it is the nation's largest single-campus medical school.

Wayne State's physician faculty provides $50 million in uncompensated care every year, or about $70,000 per faculty member. This is praiseworthy and fills a great need in our community, but considering the steady decrease in government support for such care it also is altruism that cannot be sustained. A growing uninsured population is producing a simultaneous rise in the demand for uncompensated care; at the same time, costs of care of any sort are skyrocketing and reimbursements, especially those from Medicaid and Medicare that primarily help support major urban hospitals, are declining.

Foreword

The Voices of Detroit Initiative (VODI) was our community's response to this problem and is designed to be integrated into what we trust will be an eventual national solution. The VODI Intervention Model clearly describes a process that moves toward health care reform and a strategy for organizing a delivery system specifically for people without health insurance. This book is an excellent description of the way in which local communities can come together to meet the health needs of their most vulnerable citizens. It should stimulate lively discussion as an important model for this nation as a whole as we seek ways to care for the uninsured and underinsured effectively, economically and with compassion.

Irvin D. Reid
Wayne State University
President

Foreword

Taking Care of the Uninsured: A Path to Reform

Perhaps the most challenging issue for the United States is the growing number of uninsured and underinsured Americans. These populations are less likely to receive preventive and screening services, are less likely to have a medical home, are more likely to use the emergency room, are less likely to have chronic conditions managed appropriately, and are at increased risk of dying.

Committees all over the country have devised local solutions to address the issues but very few can point to significant successful solutions. One exception has been the Voices of Detroit Initiative (VODI). VODI demonstrates what can happen when a community unites to proactively and collaboratively provide cost effective access to quality health care for its most vulnerable residents.

The elements of VODI's model (collaboration, coordination, coverage, and care) provide the compass for their work. The book describes the barriers encountered in each element, the lessons learned that can be applied in every community, and the policy changes needed for real reform.

The authors have demonstrated the impact a dedicated group of individuals can have in one community. Their book serves as a testimony to their success and will serve as a guide for others seeking a "path to reform."

Gail L. Warden
President Emeritus
Henry Ford Health System

Acknowledgments

Taking Care of the Uninsured: A Path to Reform

The Voices of Detroit Initiative (VODI) owes a great deal to the vision and guidance of the Honorable Kwame M. Kilpatrick, Mayor of the City of Detroit and former Mayor the Honorable Dennis W. Archer, chairmen of its Oversight Committee/Board of Directors. Immense gratitude is also extended to the entire Oversight Committee for their participation and leadership. During the project period members included David Campbell, Arthur Porter, MD and Michael Duggan of the Detroit Medical Center; Gail Warden and Nancy Schlichting of Henry Ford Health System; Anthony Tersigni, Ed.D and Elliot Joseph of St. John Health; John B. Waller, DrPH and Robert Frank, MD of Wayne State University; Jacqueline Majors, Kathy Harris, DrPH and Judith Harper West of Advantage Health Centers; Ricardo Guzman of C.H.A.S.S.; Mary Stephens Ferris and Wayne Bradley of Detroit Community Health Connection; James Buford, Noble Maseru, DrPH and Phyllis Meadows, PhD of the Detroit Health Department.

VODI owes the W. K. Kellogg Foundation its deepest gratitude for having the foresight to initiate the Community Voices Program and for their support and investment over five years. VODI acknowledges the following Kellogg Foundation representatives: William Richardson PhD, Gloria Smith PhD, C. Patrick Babcock, Henrie Treadwell PhD, Marguerite M. Johnson, Barbara Sabol, Terri Wright, Kay Randolph-Back, Carol Laird, Annette Beacham and Teresa Odden.

A special thanks to Ascension Health for their significant ongoing, in-kind and financial contribution to this initiative.

Special thanks to Wayne State University and the Wayne State University Press for their assistance and support for making this book possible: Irvin

Acknowledgments

Reid, PhD, Nancy Barrett, PhD, Robert Mentzer, MD, Robert Frank, MD, and Jane Hoehner.

Special thanks are also extended to consultants on the book Sungwoo Lim, Robert Ert and Devesh Twari. Also thanks to all the reviewers of our book for their editing and review comments.

A heart felt thanks to the families of the co-authors for their unwavering support through the many years it took to complete this project and this book.

The Voices of Detroit Initiative also reflects the hard work, dedication, and insight of its numerous community partners. Without the contribution of the following stakeholders, the Voices of Detroit Initiative (VODI) would not have been possible. Below are listed members of the VODI collaborative.

Chris Allen, Tonya Allen, Lila Amen, Andy Anderson, Vernice Davis Anthony, David Bach, Stacey Bailey-Johnson, Lynda Baker, Sharon Baskerville, Christine Beatty, Karen Beger, William Berk, MD, Jamillah Berry, Zeina Berry, PharmD, Milo Bishop, Rick Blakeney, Wilma Brakefield-Caldwell, Paul Bridgewater, Kelly Brittain, Anne Brown, Shelby Brown, Joyce Brown Williams, Mary Burkhardt, Michael Byrd, Rita Canty, Sharon Castro, DDS, Sharon Castronova, DDS, Frank Castronova, PhD, Elizabeth Clements, Cheryl Coleman, Ron Coleman, Kathleen Conway, Rosetta Cooper, Jeannette Davis, Nancy Degroote, Jorge Delva, PhD, Sonya Denham-Range, Andrew Dignan, Margaret Dimond, Camilla Doniver, Denise Dowell, Audrey Ector, Missy Edwald, Kirt Edward, Roy Elrod, MD, Margaret Endres, John Esselink, Ronald Evans, DDS, John A. Fairman, Haifa Fakhouri, Kristin Finton, Gerald Fitzgerald, Coit Ford III, Leonara Frazier, Nancy George, Paul Giblin, PhD, Barbara Gonzales, Amanda Good, Selma Goode, Carol R. Gove, Douglas Graham, Princella Graham, Charles Gray, Karen Gray Sheffield, Margaret Green, MD, Robbya Green-Weir, Denise Griggs-Konte, Thelma Hall, Doug Halladay, Adnan Hammad, Sandra Harris, Lisa Hartsock, Lynette Harvey, Isa Hasen, Pam Herrara, Yolanda Hill, William Hilliker, Sherry Hirota, Amanda Holm, Connie Houin, Betty Howard, Mary Ellen Howard, Gloria Howze, Sandy Hudson, Reverend Risarge"Reggie" Huff, Matt Hussman, Wendell Hutson, David Ippel, Amid Ismail, Dr.PH, Calvin Jackson, Charles Jackson, Delphine Jackson, Edna Jackson, Kenyetta Jackson, Jed Jacobson, DDS, Ifetayo Johnson, Judith Johnson, Robert Johnson, Parada Jordan, Reverend Joseph Jordan, Roslyn Joseph, Kevin Jusecxyk, Talib Kafaji, PhD, Lee Kallenbach, PhD, Jerutha Kennedy, Ram Kannan, Anthony King, Paul Kramer, Anahid Kulwicki, DNS, Beverly Lemle, Susan Levy, Cecelia Lewis, Donna Lewis, Nancy Lewis, PharmD, Richard Lichtenstein, PhD, Melany Mack, Mary

Ellen Mays, Renee McCune, Polly McGreevy, Sheryl McGrill, Bishop Milo, Pamela Moore, Anita Moncrease, MD, Michael Morgan, Si Nahra, PhD, Deborah Nicholas, Debra Nixon, Janet Olszewski, Mary Paspalas Barrett, Pamela Paul-Shaheen, DrPH, Lori Payne, Abbey Phelps, Donald Phillips, Donna Pierce, Deborah Pollard, Renate Pore, Wayne Powell, Deana Rabiah, Kannan Ramsey, Olivia Ramsey, Sonja Rashed, William Ridella, Deborah A. Ring, Mona Rizk-Ibrahim, DDS, Portia Roberson, Jessica Rose, Lovell Ross, Abby Rosenthal, Katherine Rowe, Zachery Rowe, Oliver Rue, Lisa Rutledge, Sharon Schilling, Barbara Selden, Deirdre Shires, James Shyrock, Audrey Smith, Alberta Smith Plump, April Spraggins, Christine Steverson, Robin Storey, Randy Stuck, Anne Sullivan Smith, PhD, LaJuan Taylor, Jacqueline Thomas, Terence Thomas, Pamela Wilson-Travis, Karen Trompeter, Marilyn Troublefield, Darlinda Smith VanBuren, John R. C. Wheeler, Patricia Williams, Richard Vollmerhausen, John B. Waller, Jr., DrPH, DeWayne Wells, and Elizabeth Whitley.

Although many contributed to this project and book, the authors alone remain responsible for its content and conclusions.

Preface

Taking Care of the Uninsured: A Path to Reform

Millions flock to the United States each year in hope of a better life. In this land of opportunity, it is unsettling and embarrassing that almost 50 million Americans are without health insurance, and lack access to timely, cost-effective and quality health care. The majority of these individuals are working in jobs that provide inadequate or no health care benefits. While there is considerable consensus and agreement on the need for reform leading to universal coverage, there is little agreement on how a universal health care system would be structured, financed and managed. As the baby boomer population ages and the number of uninsured continues to rise, many live sicker and die younger due to fragmented, untimely, and/or no access to needed care in a country that claims to have the best medical care available in the world. This lack of consensus extends to the current debate between Congress and the President regarding an extension of the insurance program that insures children. Immediately insuring children is a relatively small and very necessary step in the effort to provide health insurance to all Americans.

A national solution to this predicament is not imminent. This great and rising need to take care of the uninsured is made more difficult by the many competing interest groups. They add a level of complexity that hinders consensus on an approach and funding mechanism for substantive health care reform and universal coverage.

Under these conditions, many states and local communities have taken a leap of faith and stepped forward to respond to the needs of their communities and developed systems and approaches to improve access to care for the uninsured. The city of Detroit has accepted and acted on the challenge of taking care of the uninsured. We are pleased that in Detroit, health care providers, government and community leaders took an aggressive approach toward caring for those without health insurance living within our city. To that end, the Voices of Detroit Initiative (VODI) was born. The results and outcomes of this initiative have confirmed for this community that together we can take care of the uninsured and improve the health and quality of life of uninsured citizens. We have done this even while the national debate on how to take care of the uninsured rages without a clear solution. Through a city-wide collaborative partnership and with the support of W. K. Kellogg Foundation, over 33,000 low-income uninsured individuals were successfully provided coverage and access to the full continuum of health care by means of the VODI project. All of this occurred with a minimal amount of additional infrastructure funding. This book is written to provide the details of this experience, including quantitative and process outcomes of this successful local approach to taking care of the uninsured.

It is our hope that policy-makers will be informed and inspired by our experience here in Detroit and use it to tenaciously and persistently push forward until they find a way to create access to comprehensive health care for all Americans. It is our hope that health care providers can take from this experience the courage and resolve to modify their systems of care, resulting in more cost-efficient and better ways to provide care to as many as possible with existing resources while advocating for a solution that covers everyone. It is our hope that the uninsured and communities where they live will be inspired to raise their voices even louder and not give up until their health care needs are met and sustained with the implementation of a cost effective community-centered plan. It is our goal that readers will look at the results of the VODI Intervention Model as a demonstration that an appropriate system of care for all can be and must be achieved.

We wish to thank all of the many individuals and organizations who contributed to the success of this initiative. Without them our community would have never realized our *path to reform*. Their names are listed in the acknowledgements.

James D. Chesney, PhD
Herbert C. Smitherman, Jr., MD, MPH, FACP
Cynthia Taueg, BSN, MPH, DHA
Jennifer Mach, MD, MPH
Lucille Smith, MEd

Contents

1

Answering the Call:
Providing Care to the Uninsured

Since the passage of Medicare and Medicaid in the mid-1960s, the policy debate over health care reform has focused largely on who should pay and how much it will cost, rather than broader concerns about how the nation's health care delivery system can be optimized and health status improved. From President Harry S. Truman to the current administration, the underlying assumption behind U.S. health care policy has been that once a financing structure can be established and insurance models put in place, the optimal care, access, and delivery systems will naturally follow. This emphasis on cost is a result of both the high cost of health care and agreements between the policy makers and providers that built our government insurance programs. An element of this consensus between policy makers and providers remains the foundation for Medicare today: The government can pay for health care, but it may not control the delivery of health care. In order to garner provider support, policy makers relinquished control of the health care delivery system in exchange for expanded coverage.[1]

This separation of health care finance and delivery systems has remained in place for more than forty years, and it has persisted largely unquestioned. At the highest levels of political rhetoric (presidential and congressional races), the health policy debate is about cost, coverage, payment, and risk. The debaters still assume that if costs can be controlled and people covered,

---

1. Jonathan Oberlander, The Political Life of Medicare (Chicago: University of Chicago Press, 2003), 8, chap. 2.

then the problems of access, quality, and health status improvement will be solved. Even personal responsibility is often framed in financial terms. For example, questions such as who is responsible to pay for the financial consequences of personal tobacco use are part of the debate. Problems and solutions focus on who is covered by insurance and how much of that cost should be borne by the government. By limiting the scope of the debate, we ignore solutions that have a significant chance to improve health status, expand access, and drive down costs for all Americans.

The Voices of Detroit Initiative (VODI), a five-year W. K. Kellogg Foundation funded demonstration project, sought to change this paradigm. The premise going into this project was that in order to create a path to health care reform, particularly for those without health insurance, we must simultaneously address, integrate, and solve the three components of health care reform: 1) financing, 2) organizing the delivery system, and 3) facilitating behavioral and lifestyle change among patients and communities. By integrating these three components at the local level using a collaborative approach, we can move communities toward improved health status and foster a well-functioning health care delivery system. There can be no comprehensive solution toward improved access, quality, cost reduction, and health status improvement without addressing these three components of health reform simultaneously.

The findings of the VODI demonstration project allow us to glimpse the results of real health care reform. Its success reveals what can happen when a community unites to proactively and collaboratively provide cost-effective access to quality health care for its most vulnerable residents. The VODI model moves beyond the premise that simply financing health care without organizing the delivery system and facilitating behavioral and lifestyle changes will succeed at improving quality, decreasing cost, or increasing access.

The VODI story is a remarkable account of how a local community of health providers decided to *take care of the uninsured*. As in other urban and rural communities, the plight of the uninsured in Detroit is harsh. Their access to timely and coordinated health care is sporadic at best and nonexistent at worst. Consistent with the findings of the Institute of Medicine, the uninsured in Detroit are more likely to live sicker and die younger than their insured counterparts.[2] Like many communities around the country, Detroit, which has no public hospital and no financing mechanism to pay for indigent care, has struggled to provide care to growing numbers of

---

2.   Committee on the Consequences of Uninsurance, *Care without Coverage: Too Little, Too Late* (Washington, DC: National Academy Press, 2002).

uninsured. During the time of the demonstration project, uncompensated health care costs for the major Detroit providers caring for the uninsured rose to $350 million annually. These costs are largely attributable to declining insurance coverage, rapidly rising rates of chronic illness in Detroit, rising health care costs and declining primary care resources. These factors have resulted in higher rates of emergency room utilization and more avoidable hospital admissions—and therefore higher costs. Could the $350 million be spent more effectively?

Detroit's provider community decided to take a leap of faith and find out what courageous innovative action could accomplish if Detroit's health care providers banded together. To *take care of the uninsured*, Detroit providers came together and agreed to provide care to 27,500 uninsured Detroiters, approximately 13.75% of the city's uninsured population. They agreed to do so without additional reimbursement—essentially controlling for the cost of care—in order to demonstrate the value of managing care for the uninsured. The belief was that by providing health care services—specifically, primary care and medical home services—to uninsured Detroiters at no cost or at a significantly reduced cost, we could increase access to primary care and prevention services, reduce preventable hospitalizations, and decrease high emergency room use, thereby reducing the city's rapidly escalating uncompensated care costs. These beliefs needed to be tested. Therefore, the providers sought to build a model that transitioned our community to more care-effective and cost-efficient primary care and prevention services.

In the end, VODI achieved its objectives. The results were nothing short of miraculous for many of the people who received care, as David's story (see sidebar) illustrates. Our hope is that the lessons we learned and the policy recommendations we developed can help other communities, providers, and policy makers improve care for the uninsured, and thus all Americans. This book is another piece of the puzzle of *"taking care of the uninsured and a path to reform."*

> *David, a 29-year-old man who had previously been healthy and employed, suddenly became acutely ill, requiring emergency surgery. As a result of his surgery, a colostomy was necessary. Because David could not work following his surgery, he was laid off from his job and lost his insurance coverage. He had no money to pay for new coverage. For 18 months, David went from provider to provider, trying to get an assessment of his condition and schedule follow-up surgery to repair his colostomy. Without insurance, and no money to pay for his "non-emergency" colostomy repair, his pleas for help went unanswered. Even the primary care center where he sought help had no way to help David get the surgery.*
>
> *David enrolled in the VODI program, and through one of its established networks, he was provided access to the full continuum of care. Within one month of his enrollment, David's colostomy repair surgery was completed. Six months later, he was well and employed, though he remains uninsured. He wrote a letter to the VODI enrollment network coordinator expressing his tremendous gratitude for giving him his life back. For this young man, the VODI intervention was life changing.*

The process of transitioning people to an organized system of coverage and care is a continuum that moves them from coverage to health service use. This continuum is depicted as a road map in Figure 1.1. During the five-year (1999-2004) demonstration, VODI covered 25,373 uninsured individuals in Detroit by helping them obtain public insurance or by enrolling them in the VODI program. A total of 6,535 people were identified as eligible for public insurance programs, and applications for those individuals were filed. Of the remaining 18,838 VODI enrollees, 15,241 enrollees had their care tracked for at least 12 months. Of those tracked, 8,585 used services within 12 months of enrollment and became active enrollees.

Figure 1.1. The VODI Road Map

Transitioning From Uninsured to Service Use

Figure 1.2 puts the study population into context by showing the total Detroit population, Detroit's total uninsured population, the current VODI covered population, and the study population. VODI continues today, and as of January 2007, VODI has provided coverage for 33,093 uninsured Detroiters, well in excess of the initial goal of 27,500.

Figure 1.2. VODI Target and Study Populations

VODI Target & Study Populations

VODI Target Population

Detroit Population 2000	**990,992**
# Detroit Uninsured, 2000	**200,000**
Jan. 2007 YTD VODI Covered	**33,093**
5 yr. (1999 to 2005) VODI Enrollment Target	**27,500**
VODI Study Population (2000–2004)	**25,373**

VODI Study Population 2000–2004

25,373	Total # of uninsured covered by VODI intervention model, (1999–2004)	Chapter 1
18,838	VODI Enrolled & Tracked Did not have a full 12 months of service data	Chapter 2
15,421	VODI Enrolled and Tracked Did have a full 12 months of service data	Chapter 3
8,585	VODI Enrolled, Tracked, & Used Service	Chapter 4
1,448	VODI Enrolled, Tracked & Eligible for Disease Management with service data	Chapter 5

The goal of the VODI project was to improve access to care and reduce the cost of care for the uninsured in Detroit by providing a seamless and organized system of care that would set the stage for more effective and efficient coverage and delivery systems. At the intersection of the coverage and delivery systems is the "medical home" (see Figure 1.3). The assignment and use of a medical home was designed to provide each VODI client with a professional caregiver who would provide and coordinate preventive, primary, secondary, and tertiary care (The medical home is specifically defined in Chapter 2). The medical home is located at the intersection of the coverage and delivery systems because the assignment, which links a patient to a medical home, is a function of the coverage system, while the use of the medical home is a function of the care system. The VODI Intervention Model clearly links coverage and delivery in the context of a collaborative partnership.

Figure 1.3. VODI Intervention Model

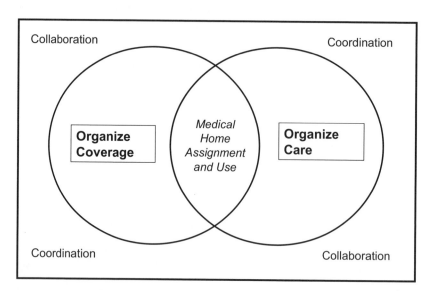

The basis of this model is that as collaboration and coordination among health care providers becomes stronger and more robust, this facilitates improved integration and organization of health care financing (coverage) and the delivery system (care).

Background

For the past decade, Detroit has weathered an economic storm that has eroded its health care safety net. In Michigan, towns from Greenville to Detroit have experienced economic decline tied to the loss of manufacturing jobs, which once offered high pay and health benefits. Bankruptcies in the airline and automobile industries have fuelled this trend. Many companies have sought to avoid bankruptcy by reducing their workforces and by trimming pension and health care benefits for their remaining employees. The number of vulnerable communities and individuals is growing nationally. Communities in Texas and California, for example, are seeing waves of undocumented immigrants crossing their borders, straining an already under resourced U.S. health care system. The Gulf Coast is challenged with rebuilding in the aftermath of Hurricane Katrina. Jacob Hacker, a Yale University political scientist, argues that middle-class families are entering a state of insecurity as the public–private retirement and health systems erode.[3]

---

3.   Jacob Hacker, *The Great Risk Shift: The Assault on American Jobs, Families, Health Care, and Retirement— And How You Can Fight Back* (New York: Oxford University Press, 2006).

As a result Michigan has been disproportionately and uniquely affected by the economic downturn in the overall U.S. economy.[4] Michigan's unemployment rate has typically led the nation. Increasing unemployment and the associated decrease in employer-sponsored health insurance, rising health care costs, and fiscal constraints on public health insurance coverage are just some of the reasons for the increasing numbers of uninsured nationally, statewide, and especially locally in Detroit. The resulting rise in the uninsured continues to place significant pressures on the U.S. health care delivery system. These pressures are driving the U.S. health care crisis by superimposing on the health care system a continued rise in demand for care. With no overall coordination, growing costs, and marked disparity in access and outcomes in health care, there is growing dissatisfaction with the U.S. health care delivery system.

Although many factors are having a negative impact on the U.S. health care system, the crisis is even more significant among safety net providers—those providers that predominantly provide care to the under and uninsured.

Nationally, the number of people without health insurance is estimated at about 50 million. A study conducted by the Commonwealth Fund in 2006 reported that about one-half of the uninsured are full-time employees, and two-thirds live in a household with an employed person.[5] Frighteningly, the lack of insurance is growing fastest among middle-income Americans.

These trends accelerated in Detroit during the 1990s, resulting in dramatic rises in the number of uninsured and uncompensated health care costs. Detroit has the largest number of uninsured of any single city in the state of Michigan. An estimated total of 200,000 people lack health insurance, and the city's health status indicators are roughly 40% poorer than the rest of the state. In addition, Detroit has no public hospital and no tax mechanism for the public funding of care for the uninsured and indigent.[6] The increasing number of uninsured has resulted in rising uncompensated care costs and, in turn, rising premiums for local corporations. Rising health care costs are making corporations less competitive in the global economy, leading to layoffs and higher numbers of uninsured. The cycle is clear; breaking the cycle means addressing the financing, coverage and care of the uninsured. Breaking the cycle begins with collaboration at the local level.

---

4. Mitchell Bean, *State of Michigan Budget Process and Outlook* (Lansing: Michigan House Fiscal Agency, 2006).

5. Sara Collins, Karen Davis, Michelle M. Doty, Jennifer Kriss, and Alyssa L. Holmgren, Filling Gaps in Health *Insurance: An All-American Problem* (New York: Commonwealth Foundation, 2006).

6. Detroit Health Care Stabilization Work Group, "Strengthening the Safety Net in Detroit and Wayne County," http://www.michigan.gov/documents/ReportofDetroitHealthcareStabilizationWorkgroup_1_70764_7.pdf.

In 1995, political and health care leaders came together to address the health and economic problems faced by the Detroit community. The drivers for these conversations included acutely rising uncompensated health care costs, rising uninsured, declining Medicaid reimbursement, the relationship between the health care systems (the second largest employer in the city) and economic development, health disparities and minority vendor purchasing initiatives. In the final analysis, these leaders realized that Detroit's uncompensated care burden could not be sustained and would erode Detroit's long-term economic development and health status if left unaddressed. They also concluded that our community had no current coordinated solutions for those without health insurance and the resulting uncompensated care burden. This collaboration led to a consensus for the need to build an effective sustainable solution—an effective path to reform.

Over the course of the next two years the ground work was laid for implementing a sustainable solution. The breakthrough came in 1997 when the W. K. Kellogg Foundation, issued a national challenge to participate in its Community Voices Initiative. This initiative was the catalyst that ultimately rallied our loosely affiliated collaborative to finally come together and apply for a Community Voices grant. The Kellogg Foundation funded 13 cities out of 80 that applied for its grant. Detroit was one of those cities.

The Kellogg Foundation's Community Voices initiative sought to provide a voice for the uninsured while investing in community partnerships that would improve access and strengthen safety net providers. The Community Voices Initiative represented a reaffirmation of the Kellogg Foundation's belief in community-driven change and partnerships. The foundation also believed that system change would require groundwork and preparation. The Community Voices Initiative expected to achieve four outcomes:

1. Sustained increases in access to care for vulnerable populations

2. Strengthening of the community safety net

3. Building of cost-effective and high-quality delivery systems

4. Development of best practices that could be
    shared with other communities[7]

The Kellogg Foundation awarded $5 million over five years to the VODI project to "demonstrate how to sustain safety net providers through partnerships with community and health and human service providers."[8]

---

7.   W. K. Kellogg Foundation, *More Than a Market: Making Sense of Health Care Systems* (Battle Creek, MI: W. K. Kellogg Foundation, 2002).

8.   Award letter from Dr. Henrie Treadwell to Mr. Gail Warden, July 7, 1998.

Former Detroit Mayor Dennis Archer's understanding of the city's critical need to have a strong health care system in order to attract business, provide employment (health care organizations are the second-largest employer in Detroit), and improve public health, provided the political impetus that brought the Detroit health system leadership to the table. His leadership prompted the CEOs of Detroit's health systems to agree to collaborate and jointly apply for the Community Voices grant. The Voices of Detroit Initiative was the result of these efforts.

The VODI project began with two major assumptions. First, the health care system does not work for everyone, especially those without health insurance, those on the margins, and the safety net providers they turn to for care. Second, by listening to those without health insurance and building community partnerships, real local solutions could emerge.

However, in the period between the groups' efforts to write the proposal for the Kellogg funding and the receipt of the grant, financing for health care dramatically changed. The federal government passed the Balanced Budget Act of 1997, which reduced Medicare and Medicaid funding, and the state instituted a full Medicaid Managed Care Program starting in southeast Michigan in 1999. The Michigan Medicaid Managed Care Program reduced Medicaid reimbursements to the state by $400 million and by $100 million in the counties around Detroit.[9] For more information on the context in which the VODI project was implemented, please refer to Appendix A, which details the economic and health status present in the Detroit area during this time period.

In the face of these policy changes, the concern was: how could health care for the uninsured be preserved and even strengthened? This book describes how Detroit's safety net providers came together to provide health care for the uninsured. The effort in Detroit took place on two levels. The first was the collaboration itself. Detroit's safety net providers listened, learned, and deliberated action steps to improve access and care for the uninsured. The second level encompassed the action steps that were implemented to identify and monitor care for the uninsured in a virtual health plan. The vision for providing health care to the uninsured started with *listening* to the uninsured.

Listening to the uninsured provided a catalogue of problems. For many people, an adverse event with health consequences can begin a downward economic as well as health spiral. At VODI's first annual meeting, participants watched a video produced by VODI in which people without health insurance told their stories. One woman in the midst of having a

---

9.   Bean, *State of Michigan Budget Process and Outlook.*

stroke told ambulance personnel not to take her to the emergency room because she was uninsured and could not afford to pay for the ambulance ride. Another person explained how a random act of violence—he was shot in the foot—had not only cost him his job but, because he lacked adequate health insurance, resulted in a disability that prevented him from getting another job. To make matters worse, the man missed his daughter's wedding because he could not work to earn travel money and could not get health insurance to obtain proper treatment for his foot. Another man without health insurance, who had experienced a heart attack, talked about reducing his daily heart medication to every other day because he could not afford to pay for his medication as prescribed. As a result this man ended up in the emergency room and was admitted to the hospital because of a preventable progression of his illness. Hearing these VODI clients, it is easy to understand how people, families, and communities face significant burdens when they lack health insurance.

The problems faced by those without health insurance have been carefully documented and analyzed. The six-volume report produced by Institute of Medicine's Committee on the Consequences of Uninsurance clearly documents the individual, family, community, and national consequences that result from the lack of health insurance.[10] Subsequent studies by the Commonwealth Fund and the Robert Wood Johnson Foundation have documented gaps in service and coverage for the uninsured—mostly the working poor who fall into the gap between eligibility for publicly supported insurance and jobs without employer-based health insurance.[11] The uninsured face reduced access to health care services and suffer poorer health outcomes compared to the insured population. The Commonwealth Fund study showed that uninsured people have large gaps in primary care and preventive services.[12] The Institute of Medicine committee concluded that these consequences are the result of fragmented finance and delivery systems for the uninsured.[13] Therefore, the VODI demonstration project began by asking a question: What would happen if care for the uninsured

---

10. Committee on the Consequences of Uninsurance, *Coverage Matters* (Washington, DC: National Academy Press, 2001); *Care without Coverage: Too Little, Too Late; Health Insurance Is a Family Matter* (Washington, DC: National Academy Press, 2002); *A Shared Destiny: Community Effects of Uninsurance* (Washington, DC: National Academy Press, 2003); *Hidden Costs: Value Lost* (Washington, DC: National Academy Press, 2003); *Insuring America's Health: Principles and Recommendations* (Washington, DC: National Academy Press, 2004).

11. State Health Access Data Assistance Center, University of Minnesota, "Shifting Ground: Changes in Employer-Sponsored Health Insurance," May 2006, http://covertheuninsured.org/media/research/ ShiftingGround0506.pdf.

12. Collins et al., *Filling Gaps in Health Insurance.*

13. Committee on the Consequences of Uninsurance, *Hidden Costs: Value Lost.*

were provided in a less fragmented system, with unfettered access to primary care and integrated services across the continuum of care?

Any strategy to reduce fragmentation must begin by bringing safety net providers together in an effort to reduce the horizontal and vertical divisions in care (see figure 4.2). A less fragmented vertical system of care for the uninsured requires independent organizations that deliver services at one end of the continuum of care to partner with organizations that deliver services further along the continuum. This strategy requires building partnerships that comprise public health departments (health education and preventive services), community clinics (primary care services), specialists and hospitals (acute, emergency, and specialty services). Horizontal integration requires competitors that provide care at the same level on the continuum coordinate their care for the uninsured. In the VODI project, this proved to be an extremely challenging step and took much longer than anticipated. Building mechanisms for horizontal and vertical integration is discussed in Chapter 2 and impacts are discussed in Chapters 3 and 4.

Payment information sources on the uninsured are also fragmented. The uninsured are the largest underserved population, but they are virtually impossible to track across providers. The financing and delivery of care to this population is not well documented or understood because the payment stream is not tied to individual patient care. Funds are provided to disproportionate share hospitals, Federally Qualified Health Centers (FQHCs), and public health departments for the care of a population, not individuals. As a result of this payment mechanism, care for uninsured patients is not necessarily tracked through the normal billing systems of health providers.

Fragmented sources of information have significant policy implications. For example, two important experienced-based measures are impossible to calculate for uninsured patients. One is the measurement of inefficiencies in care that result from multiple tests and services being performed by multiple providers. This is particularly important for uninsured patients with chronic conditions. The second is the measurement of preventive services. Without these measures, it is difficult to build policies that provide care efficiently and concentrate on cost-effective preventive services.

The VODI project brought together public health providers, health systems, community health clinics, and academic organizations to provide and measure a full range of services for a group of uninsured people living in Detroit. No sector in society could solve the uninsured problem alone. Rather, VODI was premised on the overlapping interest of each sector in solving the uninsured problem. Organizing the continuum of care requires the collaboration of many partners. Figure 1.4 illustrates this synergy. The continuum of care, provided by VODI lies at the intersection of the three sectors.

Figure 1.4. Voices of Detroit Initiative (VODI) Conceptual Design

VODI was designed as a partnership within the Detroit community among the City of Detroit health department, four Wayne County hospital networks (Detroit Medical Center, Henry Ford Health System, St. John Health, and Mercy Hospital), three Federally Qualified Health Centers (Community Health and Social Services, Detroit Community Health Connection, and Detroit Health Care for the Homeless/Advantage Health Centers), and the Wayne State University School of Medicine. The purpose of this partnership was to improve health care for the underserved through community empowerment, practical application of knowledge, and efficient use of resources.

The VODI project emphasized stakeholder investment in a path toward change. Our path was a local commitment to enroll 27,500 Detroit uninsured in a program, assume all the costs of enrollees' care (estimated at approximately $51 million[14] annually), track enrollees, and intervene to change their care utilization patterns by transitioning their care from

---

14.   Jack Hadley and John Holahan, "The Cost of Care for the Uninsured: What Do We Spend, Who Pays, and What Would Full Coverage Add to Medical Spending?" Kaiser Commission on Medicaid and the Uninsured, Issue Update, May 10, 2004, http://www.kff.org/uninsured/7084. (**$51,260,000 = 27,500 enrollees x $1,864 per capita annual cost of an uninsured person**)

emergency rooms and hospitals to more cost-effective primary care settings.

At the heart of VODI was a group of service providers from the Detroit area who created a formal, integrated network to provide broad geographic coverage and a range of health and social services to a portion of Detroit's uninsured. The network was designed to simulate an integrated delivery system and provide data on which patients were utilizing care and what kinds of care they were using. The registration and tracking system was a listening mechanism that allowed VODI to learn how the uninsured use care, build information used to deliberate action steps, and implement improvements aimed at reducing fragmentation.

Listening to the uninsured is only the initial step—listening must lead to action. The stakeholders in VODI agreed to deliberate and implement solutions. Two principles formed the core of this initiative:

1. Uninsured patients seen by partner health systems
    have characteristics similar to an enrolled population,
    and thus they can be managed as a group.

2. As a result, providers can control and optimize the volume and
    intensity of health care services received by the uninsured.

The VODI partners agreed to use these principles as operating assumptions. The project started by eliminating health insurance financing barriers up front. Care for this demonstration project was financed locally, essentially creating a universal health care model for the 27,500 Detroit uninsured to be enrolled in the project. Because the VODI partner organizations were already providing uncompensated care, they were able to develop a network for managing care without changing their funding patterns. Pluralistic funding sources allowed VODI to deliver care to a defined population, collect information that was used to improve care, and make policy recommendations. This agreement allowed VODI to focus on the question of whether care utilization patterns could be changed by developing a coverage/benefit model and by better organizing the delivery system.

The VODI Intervention Model

Novelist Stephen King, in his book *On Writing*, gives this advice to aspiring authors: "The only way to learn is by doing."[15] The key elements of how VODI built an intervention to provide improved access to care for the uninsured

---

15.   Stephen King, *On Writing* (New York: Pocket Books, 2000).

are outlined in the VODI Intervention Model. The model comprises four elements, or 4Cs: collaboration, coordination, coverage, and care (see Figure 1.5).

Figure 1.5. Elements of the VODI Intervention Model: 4Cs

– Organize **Collaboration**
- The framework for building agreement and commitment.

– Organize **Coordination**
- Working together in a common effort developing a common set of services and activities.

– Organize **Coverage**
- Agreement to pay for a set of benefits to a defined population.

– Organize **Care**
- The direct provision of services

| ↑PC ↓ER ↓SC/Inpatient |

PC=Primary Care; ER=Emergency Room; SC=Specialty/Ancill/Diag Care

The premise of the model is that by collaborating, coordinating, and implementing coverage and organizing care for the uninsured, VODI could improve primary care utilization and decrease inappropriate and high cost emergency room and hospital usage, thereby encouraging cost-effective care.

The first step is to organize collaboration. Collaboration requires building a partnership of agreement and commitment among the partners. This was the most challenging component of the project because many of the health systems and many of the partners coming together had previously been staunch business competitors. It took several years of working together to ultimately gain enough trust to collaborate on any issue, even care for the uninsured. The health system partners were concerned about a potential redistribution of care for the uninsured, which they feared would increase their respective financial burdens. It was and is no easy road: Collaboration requires "heavy lifting" as it relates to implementing this model effectively, and it required the longest time period of the four components. The time frame needed to achieve genuine collaboration was underestimated by all of the VODI partners, including the funder, the Kellogg Foundation. Coordination, coverage, and care cannot happen until the community comes together and develops enough trust, commitment, and cooperation to collaborate on an activity.

The second step involves organizing the coordination of collaborative activities. Coordination is the act of working together in concert with one another in a common effort—in this case, developing a common set of services and activities. Once the partners met and began the work of drafting a framework for how the partnership would function, the next step was to coordinate the different ways in which each institution would deliver coverage and care to this vulnerable population.

The third step is to organize coverage through the development of virtual health insurance. Health insurance is provided by an entity that agrees to pay for a defined set of health care services or benefits for a defined population. Implementing an insurance plan requires a financing mechanism to pay for care and a coverage mechanism to determine whose care and what care will be covered. The financing mechanism for VODI was represented by each provider's agreement to provide care under its current charity care policy. There was no coordinated payment system, and VODI patients did not receive bills for the services they received. However an encounter form was generated for each service provided to a VODI enrollee for internal tracking of service utilization. VODI provided virtual insurance because the plan was to give coverage to the uninsured without requiring a financing mechanism beyond each provider's willingness to assume the cost of care to VODI enrollees. Insurance coverage requires making two decisions: who will be eligible and what benefits will be covered. The coverage goal was to register, enroll, and track the health care of 27,500 patients without health insurance.

Finally, the last step is to organize the delivery system by transitioning from a fragmented set of resources to assembling, coordinating, and delivering care to an enrolled uninsured population. In the VODI project, this organization of care included not only the medical home assignment but also medical home use, a set of basic services including subspecialty care and hospitalization, and care management for difficult levels of chronic illness. The care model included basic services such as laboratory work, pharmacy, primary care, dental care, subspecialty care, and tertiary care provided in conjunction with all the partners for 27,500 people over a period of five years. These 27,500 uninsured individuals were slowly registered and enrolled and assigned a medical home within this care model. Enrollees consented to allow VODI to track their utilization of care both within and between systems and to collect and analyze data related to the utilization patterns of the population we were enrolling.

Evaluation

The VODI demonstration project was evaluated using an impact analysis.[16] The analysis focused on what happened to uninsured people's care after the implementation of the VODI Intervention Model. The intervention (collaboration, coordination, coverage, and care/delivery system) was expected to impact the outcomes: reduce emergency room use, increase primary care use, decrease specialty care and hospitalizations, and reduce the cost of providing care for the uninsured. The analysis was conducted using three types of variables: pre-intervention, intervention, and outcome. The analysis tested the impact of the VODI intervention on the outcome variables while controlling for the confounding factors that exist independent of the intervention such as demographic characteristics or enrollment site. All of these variables were aggregated from individual-level data. The impact analysis model is presented in Table 1.1.

---

16.   Lawrence B. Mohr, *Impact Analysis for Program Evaluation* (Chicago: Dorsey Press, 1988).

Table 1.1. VODI Uninsured Impact Analysis

Pre-Intervention Variables	VODI Intervention Model Variables	Outcome Variables
• Demographic characteristics: age, gender, race/ethnicity, employment, economic status • Clinical conditions: chronic conditions such as smoking and diabetes • Place of service at the time of VODI registration	• Enrollment • Medical home assignment and use • Provision of services through an organized system of care • Disease management	• Decrease emergency room utilization • Increase primary care utilization • Decrease inpatient and specialty service use • Improve transition from emergency to primary care services • Reduce the cost of care for uninsured

VODI's partners clearly expected to demonstrate several benefits from this project. Some of the expected benefits were as follows:

- Identification of insurance for some uninsured patients

- More appropriate use of services based on the VODI Intervention Model

  ◆ Medical home assignment and use

  ◆ Continuum of care provided to uninsured clients

  ◆ Increased primary care use

  ◆ Less sporadic engagement with the safety net system

  ◆ Decreased emergency room use

- ◆ Improved transition from emergency to primary care services

- ◆ Improved chronic disease management

- Maximization of other services, such as, dental, lab, and pharmacy

- Decreased cost per uninsured individual receiving treatment

VODI's accomplishments demonstrate a financial case for change. Detroit benefited from more than **$8 million** in grants that VODI secured from 1999 to 2004. By December 2004, VODI provided care to 12.7% of the uninsured population, or 25,373 of the 27,500 enrollee goal. In addition, VODI obtained public insurance (Medicaid/Adult Benefits Waiver) for more than 6,535 people at an estimated annual value of **$8.2 million** (based on Michigan Medicaid payment rates). VODI's coverage and care initiatives provided additional savings to Detroit's safety net providers. In fact the cost savings were considerable. There was a 26% reduction in costs of care attributable to VODI's impact on positive utilization patterns (Chapter 4). Safety net providers expected to spend $51,260,000 to care for 27,500 uninsured in Detroit. However the estimated annual saving from VODI's positive impact on utilization patterns was **$13.3 million** in cost savings (26% of $51,260,000). Total annual cost savings of the VODI project is therefore 42% ($8.2m + $13.3m/$51.2m). The annual financial value of the VODI project to Detroit is **$23.1 million** in cost savings and grants.

Outline for the Book

Chapter 1: Answering the Call to Provide Care to the Uninsured

This chapter has described the framework and partnership of commitment, cooperation, and agreement expectations and the environment for taking care of Detroit's uninsured. The chapters that follow explain the details of the demonstration project.

Chapter 2: Collaboration Coordination: Building the Intervention

This chapter outlines the process and issues that were deliberated in the process of building less fragmented health care services for the uninsured. Execution required deliberation and action on three issues:

1. Registration and data sharing

2. Care delivery and management

3. Increasing primary care capacity

These issues had to be answered in a way that would keep all stakeholders at the table and produce movement toward the project goals. This chapter describes how this was accomplished.

Chapter 3: Coverage: Creating an Infrastructure for Care

This chapter focuses on the registration and tracking of uninsured people. The project's goal was to register 27,500 clients in a system designed to manage and track their health care. VODI's registration and tracking efforts sought to create data resources for the uninsured in Detroit that would approximate the data available for the insured population. Only by mining comparable data resources can care for the uninsured be understood. This chapter addresses five questions:

1. What is the enrollment process?

2. Who was enrolled in VODI?

3. How were the services provided to enrollees tracked?

4. Did VODI provide coverage for enrollees?

5. What were the characteristics of the uninsured that used VODI coverage?

The chapter concludes with a discussion of the value of registration and tracking systems for the uninsured.

Chapter 4: Care: Organizing the Delivery System

One of the principal indicators of success for this project was the change in health care utilization patterns of program participants. The intervention outlined in Chapter 2 produced a less fragmented delivery system. This chapter discusses the impact of that intervention on the utilization of services by the registered uninsured. Four core questions are addressed:

1. Did VODI enrollees have access to the full continuum of care?

2. Was the use of services consistent with outcome goals of the VODI model? That is, did it:

    ◆ Increase primary care use

    ◆ Decrease emergency room use

- Reduce inpatient and specialty care

- Transition patients from emergency to primary care

1. Did the VODI model produce cost savings?

2. Which enrollee characteristics were
   associated with the outcome goals?

Lessons learned by the collaborative, including the benefits of the model for the uninsured and participating providers, are outlined in the conclusion.

Chapter 5: Care: Managing the Care of the Uninsured

An important component of the VODI intervention was a Disease Management Program. This program was designed to empower clients to utilize needed health care services and to learn about healthy lifestyle choices. Patients with one of four chronic conditions—hypertension, diabetes, asthma, and cancer—received disease management services. This chapter tests the hypothesis that patients who receive education about their disease and follow-up care with a primary care physician will utilize health care services more appropriately. The outcome variables analyzed include primary care use, emergency care use, and transition from emergency care to primary care. The chapter concludes with a discussion of the efficacy and challenges of disease management for the uninsured.

Chapter 6: Lesson Learned and Policy Recommendations

This final chapter reviews the lessons learned, describes the next steps for VODI, and outlines policy recommendations. Five policy issues are discussed:

1. Support for community initiatives for the uninsured,

2. A universal health coverage and care plan,

3. Funding primary care that is linked to the continuum of care,

4. Funding specialty care that helps link the continuum of care

5. Organize charity care.

2

Collaboration and Coordination: Moving from Goals to Action

The Voices of Detroit Initiative (VODI) succeeded in changing health care delivery in Detroit and providing access to basic health care services for tens of thousands of people who would not have otherwise received this care. The change that occurred organized coverage and care delivery for people without health insurance in Detroit. These successes were the result of a carefully designed structure and process. VODI built a structure that combined deliberation and execution and facilitated movement from consensus to action. The previous chapter outlined the four components of the VODI Intervention Model:

1. **Collaboration** among the provider partners

2. **Coordination** of safety net efforts on behalf of the uninsured

3. Organization of the **coverage** system

4. Organization of the **care** delivery system

This chapter will examine how, through collaboration and coordination, VODI was able to build a more organized delivery and care system for the uninsured. The VODI Intervention Model states that collaboration and coordination promotes a merging of the organized coverage and care delivery systems. This chapter will examine how this change process occurred in the demonstration project, and describes our experience in Detroit in order to provide lessons for other communities that are trying to expand access to health care for the uninsured.

The movement from collaboration to coordination is a two-step process. Figure 2.1 presents this process in two columns. Obtaining and maintaining organizations in the discussion to design and build the project is the first step. This is the deliberative phase, during which issues are discussed and agreements are reached. Step two, the execution stage, requires a mechanism to encourage partners to say what they will do and to track their progress toward those commitments. The execution phase produces results. Goals are necessary, but they are not sufficient without action; demonstration projects require an intervention.

This chapter will describe how the VODI project built collaboration and coordination, leading to agreement and execution. Figure 2.1 diagrams this process. Collaboration and coordination move partners together on issues, resulting in the organization and integration of coverage and care systems. Notice that in the diagram, as collaboration and coordination become larger, the circles move together and ultimately merge. The objective is to maximize collaboration/coordination and therefore agreement between the partners, with the result being enhanced integration and organization (merged circles) of coverage and care delivery systems. The first column illustrates how partners can come to agreement by discussing positions, interests, and issues. The second column shows that collaboration leads to coordinated action in order to organize and integrate coverage and care systems for the uninsured. Because this is a developmental model, Figure 2.1 contains three stages: pre-VODI intervention, VODI intervention, and VODI goal. As collaboration and agreement grow, so does the organization and integration of coverage and care systems.

Figure 2.1. How Agreement Leads to Execution of the VODI Intervention Model

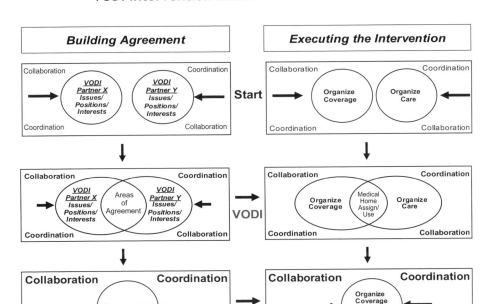

Collaboration: Building Agreement

In politics, deliberation is action.[1] Collaboration starts with deliberation, an iterative process in which individuals and groups test, challenge, and retest basic ideas and assumptions through discussion. The collaborative process requires getting the right people around the table and creating an environment of open and authentic dialogue in order to build a workable consensus. For this project, deliberation was not simply a process of seeking accurate information about the uninsured and about the safety net in Detroit, although that was important—rather, it was an opportunity for interested parties to express their ideas and their self-interest in an environment of listening, learning, and problem solving.

The purpose of deliberation is to reach an agreement on action. Jeffrey L. Pressman and Aaron Wildavsky's study of implementation concludes that "the probability of agreement by every participant in a decision point must be exceedingly high for there to be any chance at all that a program will be brought to completion."[2] The function of deliberation in this case was to

1.   James D. Chesney and Otto Feinstein, *Building Civic Literacy and Citizen Power* (Upper Saddle River, NJ: Prentice Hall, 1997), 9.
2.   Jeffrey L. Pressman and Aaron Wildavsky, *Implementation: How Great Expectations in Washington Are Dashed in Oakland* (Berkeley: University of California Press, 1973), 107.

build agreement on action steps that would reduce fragmented care for a defined population of the uninsured. The VODI stakeholders came to the table with very diverse interests, goals, resources, and commitments. The deliberative process identified and used these differences to explore realistic solutions for delivering care to the uninsured. These realistic solutions became the execution agreements, or work plans, that moved the project forward toward its goals. It took almost two years of monthly meetings at the executive and work group levels to establish real and true authentic dialogue and trust among and between the health systems, community clinics, free clinics, the public health department, and community. Based upon initial conversations, the distrust was palpable. The impact of this distrust on the change process mandated slow small steps toward change and much patience.

A workable consensus requires enough agreement by all partners to accomplish a project activity. It does not require complete agreement on every issue; it requires enough agreement for each partner to take action. In order to build a workable consensus, VODI started by gathering the right people and devising a structure that supports building agreement for action plans. The structure included work groups that built operational plans, a community advisory group that solicited community input, and policy-making groups that committed each partner to action. The structure operated in the context of a sustained commitment to the project by political and organizational leaders in Detroit. Because work group assignments were based on a consensus for action and each work group worked out its own operational details, a workable consensus was in place for most of the issues brought to VODI's policy leaders. Votes were taken to ratify decisions. The voting process allowed organizations to state their views and express the intensity of their opinions. For example, a strong negative opinion might prompt the reconsideration of an issue by a work group. In most cases after much back and forth deliberation (sometimes over months) helping to shape and re-shape policy stances, the vote on final decisions was unanimous. On a few issues around which there was controversy, majority rule decided the outcome, and VODI moved on to other issues. Change moved slowly with this process, however, each established change was sustained as we moved forward.

Getting the Right People on the Bus in the Right Seats

In his study of why some companies become great, Jim Collins comes to the realization that the transformation from good to great starts not with the vision but with getting the right people engaged and then finding the vision.[3] The process of getting VODI up and running supports Collins's conclusion. The mayor and the health system CEOs came together to solve the problem of providing health care for the uninsured. Detroit Mayor Dennis Archer; David Campbell, CEO of Detroit Medical Center; Anthony Tersigni, CEO of St. John Health; and Gail Warden, CEO of Henry Ford Health System, agreed to work together to apply for the W. K. Kellogg Foundation's Community Voices grant for Detroit. They further agreed to put their organizational resources, in the form of talented people, behind the effort to secure the grant.

The transition from agreement to action began with the writing of the proposal to the Kellogg Foundation. The application was written by a team consisting of Vernice Davis Anthony (St. John Health), James Chesney (Henry Ford Health System), Herbert Smitherman, Jr. (Detroit Medical Center/ Wayne State University), Cynthia Taueg (Detroit Health Department), and John B. Waller (Detroit Medical Center/Wayne State University). The mayor and the health system CEOs reviewed and commented on proposal drafts. The vision for VODI described in Chapter 1 was primarily the result of this collaboration. Subsequent collaboration was aided by the VODI staff, led by Lucille Smith. All of the people involved in creating VODI shared the view that providing access to care for the uninsured was a community responsibility that went beyond any single organization. They believed that their own organizations had a responsibility to act with partners to ensure access to care for uninsured citizens. It was the partnership—working in collaboration with one another and coordinating our efforts—that was the key to our success.

From the beginning, two important factors contributed to VODI's success. The people who wrote the grant application remained active and committed to the project, and this team was able to provide organizational support. People on the VODI Oversight Committee and Executive Committee had the authority in their organizations to make the resource commitments necessary to carry out implementation activities. Despite turnover at the senior level, the original grant-writing team all reported directly to their CEOs. Therefore even with senior leadership changes, the project had support and visibility at the highest levels in all partner organizations. This support and visibility translated into resources, including people, information, money, and care.

---

3. Jim Collins, *Good to Great: Why Some Companies Make the Leap—And Others Don't* (New York: HarperBusiness, 2001), 4.

If getting the right people is the first step, then building the "bus," or structure, for collaborative decision making is the second step. Initially, an Oversight Committee, Executive Committee, and Steering Committee governed VODI. This organizational structure was designed to maximize the community's input, provide a forum in which partners could discuss issues related to care for the underserved, structure the administration of VODI, and produce action toward common goals.

Figure 2.2. Voices of Detroit Initiative (VODI) Organizational Chart

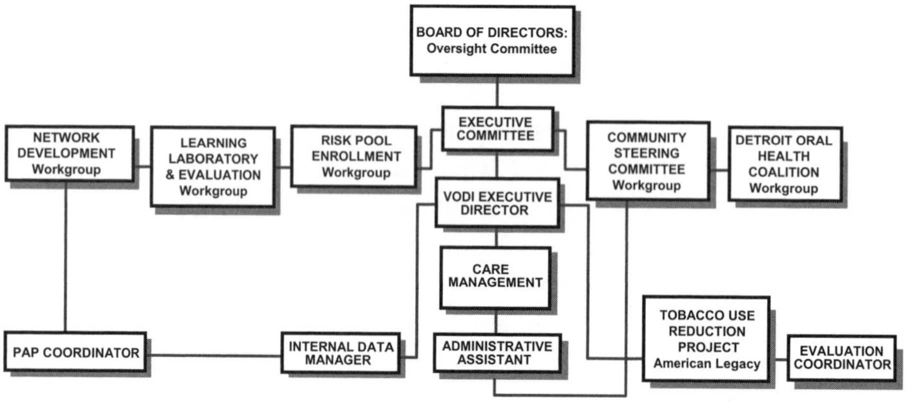

Figure 2.2 presents the VODI organization chart in 2003. The Oversight Committee was comprised of the mayor and the CEOs of the health systems. The Oversight Committee was responsible for approving policy recommendations of the Executive Committee, selecting the chair of the Executive Committee, and individually, identifying and committing their own institutional resources to the initiative. They also received quarterly reports from the Executive Committee to monitor the progress of the project.

The Executive Committee comprised representatives from the Detroit Health Department; Detroit Medical Center; Henry Ford Health System; St. John Health; Detroit Health Care for the Homeless, Detroit Community Health Connection, and Community Health and Social Services, all Federally Qualified Health Centers (FQHCs); and two community representatives elected by the Steering Committee. The Executive Committee served as the policy-making body for the project. The committee set policy and direction for the project leadership, management, budgetary and financial issues, program strategies, benchmarks, and evaluation measures. The committee was responsible for hiring and evaluating the executive director, ensuring that policies were carried out, and evaluating the performance of VODI.

The Steering Committee comprised the VODI work group leaders and community-based collaborative partners. The responsibilities of the Steering Committee were as follows:

- To elect two representatives to serve on the Executive Committee

- To review strategies identified by the work groups

- To facilitate and participate in advocacy for policy changes and strategies to achieve systemic change

The structure for strengthening community leadership in this initiative included at least two community representatives on the Executive Committee who were selected by the VODI Steering Committee. The Steering Committee comprised community-based partners:

- Consumer representatives

- Community mental health

- School system

- Seniors

- Major cultural groups (i.e., Hispanics, Arab Americans, etc.)

- Substance abuse network

- Neighborhood organization/block clubs

- Higher education

- Religious communities

The deliberative structure included five work groups. Each work group comprised representatives from the Detroit Health Department, Detroit Medical Center, Henry Ford Health System, St. John Health, Federally Qualified Health Centers (FQHCs), free clinics, and VODI staff. The work groups were charged with developing policies and procedures that would be reviewed and ratified by the Community Steering Committee, the Executive Committee, and the Oversight Committee. The five work groups focused on the following areas:

1. **Network Development:** Care models, integrated service delivery network (ISDN), and Care management/Disease management

2. **Risk Pool and Evaluation:** Risk pool registration, financing, and management of a defined population

3. **Community Steering Committee**: Engaging the community for input and guidance throughout the project including focus group training

4. **Detroit Oral Health Coalition:** Dental and Public health

5. **Learning Laboratory and Evaluation:** Research and outcomes evaluation of VODI project

The collaboration and subsequent agreements allowed VODI to have an early and positive impact on the relationship among the core partners. For example, the process of forming the partnership, defining the scope of work, and negotiating how the partners would work together resulted in a common vision for VODI members on managing the care of this population and on policy efforts. In addition, the ground rules developed at the proposal stage enabled the Executive Committee to make decisions and respond to issues in a timely fashion. This process also helped the group to identify best practices (i.e., enrollment, tracking and interfacing information systems, and creating a service network). It was important to identify the target population and then begin to manage care for that population. This allowed the initiative to maintain the current effort to care for the underserved, deliver care to a defined underserved population, and build a permanent structure for delivering and financing care to the broader population.

Coordination: Building Execution

Detroit's three health system CEOs agreed to pursue efforts to improve access to care for the uninsured in Detroit. This agreement to work together to improve access was a remarkable undertaking in light of the competitive relationship among the three health systems. Agreement on goals was necessary but not sufficient for implementation. The agreement had to lead to action and execution. Action requires accountability and transparency. Once deliberations have built agreements on strategies, a structure must be built to ensure that partners' actions are responsible, accountable, and transparent. Agreements on action steps were outlined in work plans that each partner submitted to the VODI Executive Committee. Once approved by the Executive Committee, each work plan became a contract signed by the VODI chairperson, the partner's CEO, and VODI's executive director. Each partner's work plan outlined targets for registration, data submissions, delivery system organization, uninsured care goals, community involvement, and policy advocacy actions.

The VODI Intervention Model, through its four elements—collaboration, coordination, coverage, and care—the 4Cs—proposes a single framework for increased cooperation among multiple levels of the public and private community sectors, thereby producing new opportunities and activities within whole communities, states, or nations where coalitions can take hold. Consistent with Green and Krueter's precede/proceed model of health program planning and evaluation[4] and Kretzmann and McKnight's asset-based community development model,[5] the VODI Intervention Model provides a conceptual framework of methods and procedures for building relationships and agreements within local communities for the development and implementation of action plans. It affords new opportunities and challenges for the health care community as it seeks to strengthen and organize the health care delivery system for all of its citizens. Like the Green–Krueter and Kretzmann–McKnight models, the VODI Intervention Model provides a framework that directs the initial attention to outcomes rather than inputs. This model forces planners to begin the planning process from the outcome end of the process. It encourages asking "why" before "how," and to build agreement prior to implementing an action plan. We begin with the desired final outcome and determine the agreements that are required to achieve it. Leadership guru Stephen Covey refers to this approach as "beginning with the end in mind."[6] Stated another way, the factors that are important to an outcome must be diagnosed before the intervention can be designed. If they are not, the intervention is based on guesswork and runs a great risk of being misdirected and ineffective[7].

When policy analysts look at change, they identify five action steps: 1) agree, 2) design, 3) build, 4) implement, and 5) assess.[8] These action steps build the intervention. In Figure 2.1, the text (start, VODI, goal) in the center of the diagram shows progression from VODI's beginning (pre-intervention) though VODI's implementation to the final goal. Movement

4. Lawrence W. Green and Marshall W. Kreuter, *Health Promotion Planning: An Educational and Environmental Approach,* 2nd ed. (Mountain View, CA: Mayfield, 1991).
5. John P. Kretzmann and John L. McKnight, *Building Community from the Inside Out: A Path toward Finding and Mobilizing a Community's Assets* (Chicago: ACTA Publications, 1993).
6. Stephen R. Covey, *Seven Habits of Highly Successful People* (New York: Simon & Schuster, 1989).
7. Lawrence W. Green and Marshall W. Kreuter, *Health Promotion Planning: An Educational and Environmental Approach,* 2nd ed. (Mountain View, CA: Mayfield, 1991).
8. Judith V. May and Aaron B. Wildavsky, eds. *The Policy Cycle* (Beverly Hills, CA: Sage Publications, 1978).

along the continuum requires each of the above five action steps. The action steps are sequential.

The action component at each step is very different. The agreement step requires stakeholder consensus on the goals to be achieved. It is a necessary first step because it defines the problem to be solved. During the design step, the means for solving a problem are outlined. The design must link ends and means. It must specify a solution clearly so that the partners can carry out their assigned responsibilities in subsequent steps. The build step requires the construction of the change tools specified in the design step. In this step, each partner takes responsibility for activities that further the common objective. Once built, the tool must be implemented at the production or service level (implementation step). Successful implementation requires an accountability mechanism to ensure that each partner has taken the agreed-upon action. Finally, in the assessment step, the entire process can be evaluated and further changes recommended. A vital component at this stage is transparency. Each partner shares complete information so that all partners are analyzing the same data. Information transparency helps build consensus about what works and what doesn't work and which partners are accomplishing their assigned tasks. Taking each step sequentially provides a measure of progress as the project moves toward its goals.

Each action step requires participation of the partnering agents (individuals, communities, institutions, and policy makers), allocation of resources (money, time, information, and leadership), and process (collaboration, responsibility, accountability, and transparency). Conceptually, this is captured in the action matrix (Table 2.1).

Table 2.1. Action Matrix

	Agree	Design	Build	Implement	Assess
Partnering agent action	Collaborative structure and process produces a project goal	Agents articulate a project design	Agents construct new capacity that meets the design	Responsible agents act on their assigned intervention role	Agents evaluate and redesign capacity and implementation strategies
Change process	Agents collaborate	Agents collaborate	Agents take responsibility	Agents become accountable	Agents act with transparency
Measure of success	Goal(s) agreement	Intervention designed	Capacity built	Intervention accomplished	Result documented

The change process is different at each step. Successful projects begin with collaboration, but they cannot stop there. Once collaboration has produced an agreement on what to do and how to do it, project partners must take responsibility for taking actions to achieve their common goal and work together effectively (coordination). Implementing an agreed-upon change requires that each partner's contribution to the change is measured in order to ensure accountability. Any change should be communicated to all partners to ensure transparency. Without each of these processes in place, any change is likely to run off course.

Execution of the VODI project required collaboration and coordination on three basic issues:

1. Organizing coverage

2. Organizing care delivery and management

3. Increasing primary care capacity

The process of acquiring agreement on these issues is an illustration of how VODI moved from deliberation to action. For each issue, VODI took steps outlined in the action matrix. The action steps were monitored by work plans that all partners discussed and ratified. The work plans became the vehicle that ensured collaboration, responsibility, accountability, and transparency among partners. Each issue was described by the actions that were agreed upon, the organizations that took responsibility, and the mechanisms that ensured accountability and transparency. Relationships, responsibility, accountability, and transparency, created through collaboration and coordination, are the link between agreement and execution.

Issue 1: Organizing Coverage

Collaboration
Because this initiative sought to cover, enroll, track, serve, and study a portion of the uninsured population in Detroit, the partners agreed to define a population as the focus for the initiative. Over the course of several meetings, the Enrollment and Risk Pool Work Group defined the characteristics of VODI's target population. The target population should be:

- Representative of the underserved population in Detroit (age, gender, health problems, race)

- An appropriate size so that each partner is willing to assume the cost for its portion of care for the defined population

- A mix of people who are working poor, on welfare-to-work programs, have a gap in their Medicaid coverage, and are chronically uninsured

- Large enough to provide a sample with statistically significant powers of inference

- Made up of people who are willing to participate in VODI

For the purposes of this demonstration project, the partners agreed to enroll 27,500 uninsured Detroit residents.

Each of the five partners identified enrollment volume targets, the location of enrollment workers, and a description of the enrollment and tracking process, including who would be responsible within each partner organization for this activity. Partners agreed on general guidelines and criteria, and each partner designed a process that would work in its own environment. The features of these programs were outlined in contractual work plans submitted to the Executive Committee for approval. The work plan for each health system committed to a number of enrollees, an enrollment site, and a tracking system for VODI.

The Steering Committee, Executive Committee, and Oversight Committee all reviewed and approved recommendations of the Enrollment and Risk Pool Work Group on the criteria and method for registering patients in VODI. Those deemed eligible for VODI included adult residents of Detroit who were not eligible for any other form of insurance and whose household incomes were at or below 250% of the federal poverty level.

Responsibility

Detroit Medical Center committed to enrolling approximately 10,000 uninsured over the 5 year VODI demonstration project and providing care at one of its 9 owned primary care sites and its FQHC partner's five sites. Those assigned to one of the 14 sites were given a unique identifiable VODI number that was derived from a combination of the enrollee's social security number and medical home assignment number. This number was used for tracking the place of enrollment, the medical home location, and the enrollee's service utilization patterns. The individuals presented for services at their respective primary care health center site, and their services were tracked through the center's billing system. In turn, Detroit Medical Center tracked patients by cross-matching enrollees' social security numbers against all of their encounters within its health system. However, services received at an FQHC partner site were tracked separately through that center's encounter system. Detroit Medical Center tracked both the visit volume and the site at which the patient received care. The center agreed to support the evaluation efforts of VODI and provide space for the program.

Henry Ford Health System initially committed to enrolling 7,000 uninsured patients who would be seen at Herman Kiefer Family Health Center and its FQHC partner sites. The Kiefer Center is jointly sponsored with the Detroit Health Department and serves roughly 5,600 individuals through 15,000 patient visits. Henry Ford Health System also planned to expand its enrollment efforts by recruiting enrollees from Henry Ford Hospital's Emergency Department and a Federally Qualified Health Center (Community Health and Social Services). VODI enrollees were tracked as if they were part of an insurance plan. Enrollees from Kiefer and Community Health and Social Services were tracked using a unique VODI identification number. Henry Ford Health System agreed to hire a coordinator, who operated from the Kiefer Clinic, to handle enrollment and tracking efforts.

St. John Health agreed to enroll 5,500 persons over the 5 year demonstration period who would receive care at the Northeast Health Center site, a primary care clinic that is jointly sponsored with the Detroit Health Department, at their two SJH safety net centers, their FQHC partner, and the Mercy primary care center. The emergency department at St. John Hospital and Medical Center was also an enrollment site. Discussions with patients about VODI and their participation occurred on site (clinic or emergency room visit) or during a follow-up telephone call or primary care visit. These enrollees were tracked as if they were part of a separate insurance plan.

Mercy Hospital of Detroit agreed to enroll 5,000 patients seen in its Emergency Department and care provided at the Mercy East Side Health Center. Mercy used the criteria identified by VODI to select and enroll patients. More specific system information changes were identified that allowed Mercy to track nonenrollees as well as enrollees in VODI. Mercy also reviewed its information system to determine what modifications were required in order to collect the minimum data set in an acceptable format. Mercy hospital closed at the end of the first year of the VODI project. All of the remaining VODI partners agreed to absorb Mercy's initial commitment of 5,000 enrollees. There are no data from Mercy in the VODI database. Subsequently, Mercy opened a free clinic as it continued its commitment to the community, and St. John Health became its partner. Table 2.2 summarizes the VODI Kellogg grant funding distribution and Enrollment Commitment by VODI partner for the 5-year demonstration period.

Table 2.2. VODI Kellogg 5 year Grant Funding Distribution and Enrollment Commitment by VODI Partner

Kellogg $5 million Grant Distribution by VODI Partner	VODI Partner: 5 yr. Enrollment Commitment-total 27,500
DMC Kellogg $880,226	5 year Enrollment Commitment 10,000
HFHS Kellogg $607,076	5 year Enrollment Commitment 7,000
SJH Kellogg $491, 042	5 year Enrollment Commitment 5,500
Mercy/DHWP Kellogg $409,788	5 year Enrollment Commitment 5,000
VODI Central $2.5 million	Enrollment/Registration/ Policy/System change, Network Development, Community involvement

By the end of the 5-year demonstration project, the VODI collaborative was successful in reaching its goal of providing coverage to 27,500 individuals.

Accountability and Transparency

In order to achieve accountability and transparency, VODI published monthly enrollment reports. The enrollment reports showed the progress toward each partner's enrollment goal. The reports functioned as enrollment scorecards, allowing all partners to evaluate one another's progress toward meeting the enrollment targets. These reports were presented and discussed at the monthly Executive Committee meetings. Enrollment reports made enrollment transparent, as all partners could see the others' success or failure. Partners discussed enrollment obstacles and plans to improve the enrollment process.

The enrollment and tracking system was effective. As of January 2007, VODI had screened and covered more than 33,000 individuals with enrollment of more than 25,000 into the VODI program and 7,000 into public insurance programs. VODI successfully implemented a standard application process among unrelated providers to assign a medical home and generated enrollment and utilization reports on VODI enrollees. Chapter 3 will review more completely the tracking and enrollment system and examine the characteristics of the VODI enrolled population.

Issue 2: Organizing Care Delivery and Management

Collaboration

One of the first steps that the Network Development Work Group took was to begin an inventory of local and community resources available to the uninsured. It established that the primary care capacity—including the Detroit Health Department, the Federally Qualified Health Centers, and the free clinics—had a total of 24.35 full-time equivalent (FTE) physicians, 13.11 FTE nurse practitioners, and 4.0 FTE physician's assistants[9]. This represented the total Detroit primary care safety net of providers with either a mission or a mandate to care for the uninsured. The work group also found underutilized resources, such as pharmacy and laboratory services at the Detroit Health Department. The Network Development Work Group noted that no one was tracking the utilization patterns of the uninsured. Although the committee knew that patients were traveling from emergency room to emergency room, with significant duplication of services, it could not identify these patients or track their service utilization.

As a result, the Network Development Work Group developed a list of core services, support services, and referral services that would be provided to each VODI enrollee. Community-based disease management and medical home services were also defined for the project. These core services were agreed to by the Community Steering, Executive, and Oversight committees. Defining the disease management population was necessary, as VODI partners did not have the resources to provide this service to every enrollee. After deliberation by several committees, the partners agreed that the most prevalent chronic diseases should be the starting point for disease management referrals.

The VODI Network Development Work Group also established a definition of *Health* to communicate a holistic approach to care provision. The definition was based on a modified version of the World Health Organization's definition of *Health,* proposed by Dr. Herbert C. Smitherman. This definition recognizes the individual's economic and spiritual well-being, as well as the well-being of one's community, as important factors in shaping health. By including the community, this definition underscores the composite expression of social and cultural circumstances that condition and constrain lifestyle behavior choices.[10, 11]

---

9.   VODI Detroit Safety Net Assessment Survey, May 2002
10. Constitution of the World Health Organization (WHO), United Nations, 1948. Health is defined in the WHO constitution as a state of complete physical, mental and social well-being and not merely the absence of disease or infirmity.
11. Lawrence W. Green and Marshall W. Kreuter, *Health Promotion Planning: An Educational and Environmental Approach,* 2nd ed. (Mountain View, CA: Mayfield, 1991).

VODI used the following definition of *Health*:

> Health includes the state of complete physical, mental, socio-*economic, and spiritual* well-being *of the individual and thus their community,* and not simply the absence of disease or infirmity.[12]

The Network Development Work Group next began convening those responsible for providing basic services to the uninsured together in one room. The VODI Network Development Work Group developed an overall concept to organize care for the uninsured. After numerous meetings, there was unanimous agreement that the anchor for the VODI care model would be the concept of the medical home. The medical home was defined by the group as follows:

> A medical home is not a building, house, or hospital, but rather an *approach* to providing health care that is accessible and provided in the local community; recognizes the family and/or other self-identified social support network as a care partner and the principle caregiver and has an identifiable primary health care professional who provides and coordinates preventive, primary and secondary/tertiary care, which is aligned to supportive, educational and community-based services, all concerned about the well-being of the person where the cultural background is recognized, valued, and respected.[13]

Finally, the group completed and approved a list of core medical services that would be provided to every VODI enrollee; this list was defined as the *VODI Core Services*. These core services included primary care and preventative services, laboratory and diagnostic services, health education and support services, and treatment. The basic set of services included pharmacy, laboratory, medical care, and care management. Although specialty and inpatient care were not identified as core VODI services, each provider was expected to make referrals if care was required.

---

12.   Herbert C. Smitherman, Jr. MD, "The Health Status of African-Americans in the U.S.," lecture presented at the Third African/African-American Summit, Dakar, Senegal, West Africa, April 29–May 6, 1995.
13.   American College of Physicians, *The Advanced Medical Home: A Patient-Centered, Physician-Guided Model of Health Care* (Philadelphia: American College of Physicians, 2006), http://www.acponline.org/hpp/adv_med.pdf.

Responsibility

With the agreement to serve VODI enrollees, each network partner took responsibility for its role in building a safety network to accomplish the following activities:

- Provide and manage patient care as a primary care medical home

- Provide the basic or core package of services

- Arrange for emergency, specialty, and hospital care

- Share data with the VODI program office

During the planning phase of this project, all safety net providers in Detroit were invited to participate. This group included four Detroit-based hospital systems, three FQHC agencies that had a total of six health centers, the Detroit Health Department and its two health centers, and other free clinics serving the uninsured located in the city. The program was confined to Detroit, and only these locations were invited to participate. The delivery system was organized around the hospitals into networks. There was no public hospital in Detroit or Wayne County. The networks were formed with a hospital(s) and its existing and new primary care safety net provider partners. During the early start-up phase of the program, Mercy Hospital closed and opted out of the program. The remaining three delivery systems became the focus of enrollment, service delivery, and data collection for VODI enrollees.

The care responsibilities were defined within each network. The medical home was responsible for preventive and primary care services and served as an intake point for uninsured people. The emergency room was also an intake point and provided emergency services to uninsured patients. The hospital provided specialty and inpatient services to its network registrants. Each network was responsible for transitions between providers within the network. Emergency room patients who needed primary care follow-up were sent to their assigned network medical home. Primary care patients who required specialty or inpatient services were sent to the network hospital for those services. The specific components and operation of each network are described in Chapter 4.

Accountability and Transparency

Accountability and transparency were accomplished through quantitative and qualitative status reports back to the provider partners. These reports were presented and discussed at monthly Executive Committee meetings.

The quantitative reports show how primary care emergency room, hospital, and specialty services were utilized by enrollees at 11 sites within the three networks. The reports confirmed that each network was delivering care to its enrolled population. Executive Committee minutes also showed considerable discussion of qualitative reports on use patterns and patient transitions within and between networks. Chapter 4 gives a fuller description of the networks and examines use patterns.

Issue 3: Increasing Primary Care Capacity

The VODI partners agreed to increase primary care capacity by seeking federal funds. Two vehicles were chosen to do so. First, VODI sought to increase federal funding from the Health Resources and Services Administration for additional FQHC primary care centers in Detroit on behalf of the city's uninsured. VODI calculated an immediate need to provide primary care for an additional 30,000 uninsured and underinsured people by expanding or creating new access points for the existing FQHCs. Second, VODI applied for Community Access Program (CAP) funding from the Health Resources and Services Administration, using a three-pronged proposal designed to improve access to pharmacy, oral health, and disease management services linked to primary care. Because these funding vehicles are distinct, the phases (collaboration, responsibility, accountability, and transparency) are discussed separately.

Strategy 1: Funding for Additional Primary Care Access Points

Collaboration

Movement from the desire for federal funds to actually writing proposals and receiving federal dollars required partner collaboration on issues such as the location of new access points, partnership arrangements between health systems and FQHCs, and the distribution of new funds among partners. To solve these issues, the VODI Oversight Committee created a Primary Care Task Force. The task force was charged with the following:

- Expanding primary care capacity for Detroit's uninsured

- Restructuring the relationship between the Detroit Health Department, the health systems, and the FQHCs in a way that would maximize funding for primary care and increase the efficiency and use of existing resources.

To meet these charges, the Primary Care Task Force organized discussions between FQHCs and health systems on partnerships and locations for new access points. The task force agreed to facilitate relationships among the community, government, facilities, providers, and services in order to create a sustainable, effective network of care for the uninsured. The networks were strategic affiliations of collaborating public–private safety net providers, aligned both across the continuum of care and among payers, providers, and the community. This was achieved through the integration and coordination of community-based services; prevention and health education; primary, specialty, and hospital services; administrative and management information services; finance; and care, case, and disease management. The purpose was to improve access to care, improve the quality of care, ensure the cost-effective optimization of patient care outcomes, and ultimately, improve the health status of the community.

The Primary Care Task Force agreed that there was a great need for the expansion of primary care in Detroit and recommended that all new access point applications should:

- Be reviewed by VODI for the purpose of advising on the issue of service duplication and service area overlap.

- Ensure the integration and coordination of services and the continuum of care of the new access point(s) with existing health care resources.

- Promote information sharing relative to enrollment, tracking and utilization patterns of the uninsured.

- Integrate public health–related services with primary care services at proposed sites.

Responsibility

The Primary Care Task Force minutes from September 14, 2001, clearly demonstrated that partners were solidifying responsibility for current partnerships and committing to applications for new access points. The minutes indicated four specific actions taken by VODI partners:

1. Detroit Medical Center supported the four existing Detroit Community Health Connection sites, their nine owned primary care clinics, a nurse-managed faith-based site (Imani Clinic), and one new access point in partnership with Detroit Community Health Connection.

2.   St. John Health discussed the viability of two sites with Detroit Community Health Connection (Brightmoor community) and explored a partnership with the latter for a site at St. John Community Center. After considerable discussion, Detroit Community Health Connection agreed that its interests would be best served by strengthening its partnership with Detroit Medical Center, as opposed to initiating a new partnership with St. John Health.

3.   St. John Health and Advantage Health Centers (aka Health Care for the Homeless) formed a partnership and opened a clinic in the Brightmoor community and, more recently, in northeast Detroit in 2006. As noted earlier, St. John and Mercy Free Clinic also formed an alliance. These along with two sites operated by St. John Health and one in partnership with the Detroit Health Department constituted the safety net primary care sites for this network.

4.   On December 31, 2001, Community Health and Social Services opened a new access point at Midtown in partnership with Henry Ford Health System.

Accountability and Transparency

As a result of the agreements outlined here, VODI oversaw the development of several new access point applications. VODI's first successful proposal, Community Health and Social Services Midtown, was funded the first time it was submitted. The other access points—Thea Bowman, Nolan Community Health Center, and Advantage Family Health Center—were not funded on their first submission. In fact, the Nolan Community Health Center took at least three attempts and the others at least two. More recently, applications from VODI partners have been approved more easily. This was partly attributable to a meeting of the minds with the Health Resources and Services Administration and advocacy by VODI and the Detroit community. The Health Resources and Services Administration encouraged those interested in either FQHC or "look-alike" status to seek support from VODI. The Health Resources and Services Administration understood that VODI had organized primary care for the uninsured in Detroit.[14] In 2004, VODI was recognized on the U.S. Senate floor for its work on behalf of Detroit's uninsured.[15]

---

14.   Meeting of Federally Qualified Health Centers, Michigan Department of Community Health, and VODI, Detroit Community Health Connection, 2004.

15.   2004 U.S. Senate Resolution, Senator Carl Levin of Michigan, Wednesday, September 8, 2004.

Evidence of VODI's significant success in promoting new access sites for primary care included five new FQHC primary care sites, one look-alike community health center that comprises three primary care sites, and a new FQHC organization in western Wayne County, established in partnership with Oakwood Health Care. The latter occurred after the demonstration phase of VODI ended.

Strategy 2: Community Access Program Grant

Collaboration

Pharmacy services, dental care, and disease management were identified early on as significant needs and service gaps by the Network Development Work Group and the Executive Committee. The VODI partners agreed to apply for funding to address these issues under the Clinton administration's Community Access Program (CAP). In 2000, the Department of Health and Human Services announced that VODI would receive $2.5 million over three years to implement a three-pronged approach to expanding primary care access. The federal grant was matched by an additional $1 million from Ascension Health (the nation's largest nonprofit health system) whose local affiliate, St. John Health, would be the grant fiduciary on VODI's behalf. The three prongs of the project were pharmacy access, oral health, and disease management.

Pharmacy Access

The goal of the pharmacy access program was to improve the health status of uninsured Detroit residents by providing access to free or low-cost prescription drugs. It streamlined the process of accessing pharmaceutical companies' indigent care services, reduced the costs of providing properly labeled samples, and processed pharmaceutical company indigent care program applications. The goals were achieved through the collaboration of VODI with participating pharmacy and primary care sites, as well as pharmaceutical companies that provided medications to indigent populations at lower costs.

Even before the CAP program, VODI had begun to develop an innovative pharmacy access campaign that utilized a drug replacement system. Under this program, the primary care clinics participating in VODI agreed to provide VODI clients with a prescription/voucher form that could be filled at no cost at pharmacies within the Detroit Health Department. A number of pharmaceutical manufacturers agreed to donate replacement drugs to these pharmacies. Some manufacturers also allowed VODI to take responsibility for the indigent care screening process. This streamlined the process and enabled enrolled VODI clients to receive free prescription medications in an efficient manner, thus ensuring their ongoing access to needed medications. In addition, VODI collaborated with the Detroit Health Department to put in place a robotics system for dispensing prescriptions to further streamline the provision of free or low-cost prescriptions and to operate the pharmacy access program.

Oral Health

The goal of the oral health project was to integrate oral health care into the primary care services provided by VODI providers in order to build an oral health infrastructure in Detroit and improve the employability and social health status of VODI members. The CAP grant enabled VODI to develop an educational and tracking system for oral health and to increase access to desperately needed dental health services for the uninsured. The oral health component has had three parts: development of an educational and training module for primary care providers, the reduction of disparities in dental care for at-risk populations, and the establishment of a dental workforce infrastructure to provide oral health services to uninsured Detroiters.

These three parts were achieved through the collaboration of VODI with the University of Michigan Dental School, the dental clinics of the Detroit Health Department, and St. John Health. The University of Michigan Dental School agreed to work with VODI to develop an educational and training module, and VODI agreed to participate in the University of Michigan's project examining dental care disparities. The collaboration of VODI with the Detroit Health Department and St. John Health allowed dental care services to be provided to low-income residents at these facilities.

Disease Management

The CAP dollars supported the social support and health education resources needed to sustain the medical home concept. These support services sustained the linkage of VODI enrollees with an identifiable primary health care professional who provided and coordinated preventive, primary, secondary, and tertiary care within their medical home. VODI also worked to identify which services were most needed and where gaps in the human service infrastructure existed. The implementation of the Disease Management Program required an agreement between the three health system networks and the Detroit Health Department. Disease management clients were identified from these organizations, either by direct referral from a health practitioner or by referrals from the health systems at the time of enrollment. (See Chapter 5 for more details on the Disease Management Program and screening process).

Responsibility

The activities outlined in the CAP grant were carried out by the entire VODI structure, including the Oversight Committee and the Executive Committee, which retained overall program responsibility. St. John Health acted as the grantee and financial fiduciary for the project. While VODI had primary responsibility for coordinating these activities, the organizations participating in the grant activities shared responsibilities related to the provision of services. The pharmacy, dental, and disease management components each had particular responsibilities involved.

For the pharmacy component, a number of partnering organizations assumed responsibility for providing access to free or low-cost medications for an indigent population. In addition to the participating sites and manufacturers, a Pharmacy Access Committee was added to the VODI structure to address the implementation of improved pharmacy access. Access was also improved through a system of robotics brought online during the first year of the project at the Detroit Health Department. This allowed the program to develop effective policies and procedures for optimally utilizing the robotics equipment.

For the dental component, VODI shared responsibilities with the partnering organizations or sites. VODI worked with the University of Michigan School of Dentistry to identify population subgroups that had traditionally received inadequate dental care and to determine how best to provide adequate care in the community. This occurred alongside the development of expanded dental services offered at the Detroit Health Department's dental clinic site.

For disease management, VODI maintained responsibility for the provision of the program's services. VODI staff members were hired to directly implement this initiative with advice from the Network Development Work Group and Steering Committee.

Accountability and Transparency

Federal grant requirements built a reporting structure designed for accountability and transparency. Each activity specified in the grant was measured against the goals established in the proposal. This discipline ensured action and helped grantees address unmet goals. Not only did it ensure that the federal money would be well spent, it also allowed project partners to clearly see how the project was going and who was contributing to its success.

Regular reports on pharmacy services were produced. These reports showed that pharmacy services were provided to 2,784 VODI patients during the first 18 months after the installation of the robotics equipment

(January 2002–June 2003), for a total 29,346 prescriptions. The Detroit Health Department contributed prescriptions to VODI's patients at a total cost of $790,092.86. The Detroit Health Department filled more than 196,000 prescriptions in 2003 and had 6,000 encounters. The top 20 prescriptions dispensed were for pain, high blood pressure, diabetes, asthma, cholesterol, heartburn, acid reflux disease, and ulcer.

Reports quantifying the amount of dental services were also generated. These showed that the total number of dental procedures provided to VODI patients was 1,459, while the number of total patients (VODI and non-VODI) for the dental clinic was 2,811. In all, 61% of the procedures were diagnosis related, 27% were extractions, and 7% were restorative, either crowns or partial denture. Appropriately 50% of the patients had one visit, 40% had two to three visits, and 10% had four or more visits. The median age was 38 years, down from previous years, when the average age was 40. Dental services continued to be paid for on a sliding fee basis.

The disease management component had regular reports produced for review by the VODI Executive Committee, as well as, those completed for the federal government. The impact and activities of the Disease Management Program are described in Chapter 5.

Measuring Success

Row 3 of the action matrix (Table 2.1) is labeled "measurement of success." Each stage and each issue has its own measure of success. Table 2.3 summarizes VODI's success during each stage for the three issues outlined here. For each issue, VODI's accomplishment at one stage provided the capacity to succeed at the next stage. The process is sequential. Missing one step (or not carefully accomplishing each step in order) leads to failure.

Table 2.3. VODI Accomplishments

	Goals Agreement	Intervention Designed	Capacity Built	Intervention Accomplished	Goal Documented
Issue 1 Organizing coverage	Registration criteria and targets set	Registration process designed	Registration system built, provider targets set	Uninsured covered (see Chapter 3)	Registration reports shared
Issue 2 Organizing care delivery and management	Care model and core services consensus	Medical homes identified	Delivery networks established	Care delivered to registrants (see Chapters 4 and 5)	Utilization reports reviewed and discussed
Issue 3 Increasing primary care capacity	Funds sought for FQHC expansion and CAP grant	New access points identified, CAP proposal written	New access points and CAP grant funded	New access points built and CAP grant implemented	Reports to funders and partners outlined progress

Following these steps allowed VODI to turn collaboration and coordination into more organized and integrated coverage and care systems. Outcomes for each issue broadly defined here are further analyzed in Chapters 3 (coverage), 4 (care), and 5 (care and disease management).

For communities that are trying to build programs to care for the uninsured, there are four lessons that can be drawn from the VODI experience.

Lessons Learned

Lesson 1: Getting the right people in the right structure is vital to achieving a workable consensus.

Lesson 2: If collaboration is going to lead to action, agreement is more important than the size of the step.

Lesson 3: Relationships, responsibility, accountability, and transparency—created through collaboration and coordination—are the link between agreement and execution. The key to successfully reaching goals is to balance results (completion of the task), process (how work gets done), and relationships (how people's involvement and contributions are validated and valued).

Lesson 4: Reporting mechanisms, such as benchmark-driven scorecards, improve accountability and transparency within the collaborative and move the project forward. The scorecard is a useful device for tracking and confirming progress and deliberating future actions. The discussion of scorecard results at the policy-making level helps maintain consensus and focuses action on goals.

3

Coverage: Creating an Infrastructure for Care

Mary Morris, a licensed practical nurse for 20 years, is one of VODI's success stories. Her story illustrates how health care coverage can make a difference in the lives of everyday people. We met Mary more than six years ago. She was divorced, depressed, homeless, jobless, and in poor physical health. She had slipped and fallen on the ice, sustaining a head injury—her third such injury. She also suffered from thyroid problems. She had to give up her job because of her health problems, creating financial stress. Her life began to go downhill from there: She lost her home and ended up living in her car. Major depression set in. Mary was referred to VODI. Today, Mary is on Medicare, receives disability payments, still sees her VODI medical home provider, has attained a college degree, and is currently working as a mediator for a nonprofit. Mary recently described what VODI's coverage and care meant in helping her to become a person who aspires and contributes to society: "VODI provided a nurturing system that allowed me to grow, develop, thrive, be successful and find a new professional identity. VODI's care and disease management program staff looked at me as a whole person, not just addressing my health needs, but my social needs also. They looked at my needs for food, shelter and emotional support." Although she has some new health challenges, Mary is working 20 hours a week. Her new health problems are under control because she has access to a primary care physician, and she is looking forward to returning to work full time, which will afford her health insurance and a salary of comparable worth.

Figure 3.1. VODI Intervention Model (VIM):4Cs

- Organize Collaboration
  - SJHS/HFHS/DMC/OHS/DHD/WCHD/WSU/FQHC
  - The framework & partnership of commitment, cooperation and agreement
- Organize Coordination
  - The act of working together in a common effort developing a common set of services and activities
- Organize **Coverage**
  - **Registration**
  - **Enrollment**
  - **Medical Home Assignment**
  - **Tracking**
  - **Data Collection and Analysis**
- Organize Care
  - Medical Home Use
  - Basic Services:
    - PC/Pharmacy/Lab/Dental
  - Care Management
  - Disease Management
  - Subspecialty Care
  - Hospitalization

| **↑PC ↓ER ↓SC/Inpatient** |

PC=Primary Care; ER=Emergency Room; SC=Specialty/Ancill/Diag Care

The purpose of health insurance is to provide access by creating a financing mechanism to pay for care and a coverage mechanism to determine which services and populations will be eligible for payment. Figure 3.2 presents the core elements of an insurance mechanism. The Voices of Detroit Initiative (VODI) Intervention Model sought to organize coverage for some of Detroit's uninsured. The project's goal was to enroll and care for 27,500 clients in a virtual insurance plan that was designed to manage and track the clients' health care. The term "virtual insurance" is used because although VODI organized the coverage, it did not build a new payment mechanism beyond the capacity and willingness of providers to absorb the cost of care provided to VODI enrollees. VODI sought to create a data infrastructure for the uninsured in Detroit that would be equivalent to data captured for an insured population.

Figure 3.2. Core Elements of a Health Insurance Mechanism

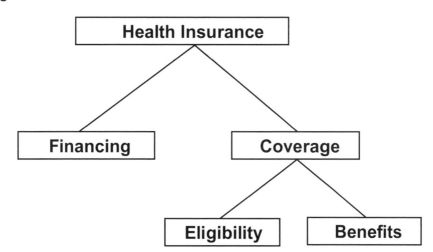

Research has shown that a major consequence of the lack of insurance coverage is that needed care is delayed or denied.[1] What we don't know is who among the uninsured will use an organized coverage system to get the care they need. A study by Erin Taylor and her colleagues begins to fill this gap. Their assessment of community coverage programs in Texas, California, and Maine concludes that participants sought coverage less for immediate health needs and more because it provided access to preventive and primary care services.[2] The question remains, who among the uninsured will use the services made available by coverage? Will the uninsured poor, employed, less educated, men, certain cultural or ethnic groups, or people with chronic conditions use an organized delivery system? These questions are at the heart of this chapter.

The VODI demonstration project was designed to build a safety network to provide high-quality, cost-effective health services to a defined enrolled population of people who are low income, uninsured, and ineligible for county, state or federal insurance programs. Numerous studies have shown that the uninsured lack access to basic services in any organized system of care. The VODI partners sought to provide access through organized networks of care that facilitate receipt of the right care at the right time and at the right place. Although a demonstration project, VODI's enrollment process was not structured in a randomized research format. Enrollment

---

1. Sara Collins, Karen Davis, Michelle M. Doty, Jennifer Kris, and Alyssa L. Holmgren, *Filling Gaps in Health Insurance: An All-American Problem* (New York: Commonwealth Foundation, 2006).
2. Erin Fries Taylor, Catherine G. McLaughin, Anne W. Warren, and Paula H. Song, "Who Enrolls in Community-Based Programs for the Uninsured, and Why Do They Stay?" *Health Affairs* 35, no. 3 (2006): 183–191.

was more or less a convenience sample of Detroit's uninsured consisting of people without health insurance, who presented for service at designed locations, including emergency rooms, met the eligibility criteria and agreed to enroll. The information system enrolled and tracked care of the uninsured. This defined population of users allowed VODI to establish a database that included health assessment, utilization, and outcome data. National surveys are useful policy guides, but they do not provide enough detail for local action and policy making. Only with local data collection structures comparable to those of an insured population can care for the uninsured be understood with a view to making changes as needed. The data collection and information system created by VODI was used to evaluate the effectiveness of network services in improving health status and providing more cost-effective care.

Ultimately, VODI's success was measured by whether patients were enrolled, care was delivered, patterns of service use changed, and lessons were learned. This chapter addresses five questions:

1. What is the enrollment process?

2. Who was enrolled in VODI?

3. How were the services provided to enrollees tracked?

4. Did VODI provide coverage for enrollees?

5. What were the characteristics of the uninsured that used VODI coverage?

What is the enrollment process?

The first operational task of VODI was to enroll people without health insurance who met the program eligibility criteria. Those eligible for VODI included adult residents of Detroit, 18-64 years old, who were not eligible for any other form of insurance and whose household incomes were at or below 250% of the federal poverty level. The eligibility criteria were designed to target the working poor—those not poor enough to qualify for government-sponsored health care insurance and who did not have an employer sponsored health care benefit.

The enrollment process consisted of two stages:

Stage 1: The first stage verified that the enrollee was not already enrolled in Medicaid or some other insurance program. The eligibility criteria required that VODI enrollment workers verify the lack of eligibility for any third party coverage particularly Medicaid or the County's Adult Benefit Waiver program (PlusCare—a Wayne County low-income insurance program) before enrollment in VODI. At the time of enrollment in VODI, enrollment workers took Medicaid and PlusCare applications to ensure that clients were not eligible. During the screening process, additional self-reported demographic and personal health information was collected. The questions included: Are you between the ages of 18 and 64? Do you meet at least one of the following conditions: blind; parent or caretaker of a minor child (under 20 years old); disabled and been unable to work for 12 months or more; and/or a physical or mental condition that prevents you from working and is expected to result in an increased risk of mortality?

To facilitate Medicaid and PlusCare applications, VODI established a partnership with the Family Independence Agency of Wayne County, the Medicaid enrollment agency in Detroit, and Wayne County's Health Insurance Bureau. The screening process revealed that the partnering primary care sites were not taking Medicaid and PlusCare applications. Instead, primary care sites were referring potential eligible patients to the Family Independence Agency. However, many of the patients never get to the agency and remain uninsured. The VODI partners agreed to take Medicaid and PlusCare applications at their primary care sites, an additional expense for the partners. The Medbury Family Independence Agency office and the PlusCare administration agreed to expedite review for all VODI client applications. The goal was to expedite the Medicaid and PlusCare process for clients who may have been eligible for those programs. The impact of this verification is summarized in Table 3.1

Stage 2: After verifying that the enrollee (patient) was not registered in another program and met the VODI criteria, the client individual was enrolled by the VODI staff and assigned a primary care medical home within one of the networks of care. All enrollees became part of the program's electronic database.

Table 3.1. VODI Clients Registered and
Screened for Insurance, 2000-2004

	Registration Year												Total
	1999		2000		2001		2002		2003		2004		
	#	%	#	%	#	%	#	%	#	%	#	%	
PlusCare/ Medicaid application filed	0	0.0	1,177	47.9	3,603	58.9	378	5.0	106	2.3	1,271	27.1	6,535
VODI enrolled	16	100.0	1,279	52.1	2,510	41.1	7,107	95.0	4,514	97.7	3,412	72.9	18,838
Total	16	100.0	2,456	100.0	6,113	100.0	7,485	100.0	4,620	100.0	4,683	100.0	25,373

The verification process was effective. Medicaid- and PlusCare-eligible people were identified, especially in 2000 and 2001. In 2001, more people were identified who were eligible for public health insurance (58.9%) than were enrolled in VODI (41.1%). This VODI driven growth in public health insurance enrollment (i.e., PlusCare) helped to reach the enrollment capacity limit of local government-sponsored insurance. As a result of the PlusCare enrollment moratorium, VODI enrollment then grew to about 90% of the people screened. The close link between uninsured and publicly insured patients is clear: When public insurance is closed or eligibility is restricted, the uninsured pool grows. As former President Bill Clinton said after the health care reform debate of the 1990s, "Universal health coverage is not rocket science. You've either got to require the employers to offer health insurance or you have to pay for it with tax money."[3] Table 3.1 demonstrates just how closely public health insurance is linked to the uninsured.

VODI enrollment screening took place as individuals presented for service. Enrollment and care coordinators located in VODI partners' primary care clinics and emergency departments contacted each individual who was uninsured and determined whether the individual qualified for VODI. The enrollment process captured the following data:

- Site's medical record number

- Insurance status

3.   Todd S. Purdum ."Striking Strengths, Glaring Failures" New York Times December 24, 2000.

- Name

- Address(es)

- Telephone number(s)

- Emergency contact information

- Social security number

- Date of birth

- Gender

- Marital status

- Ethnic background

- Citizenship

- Homeless status

- Veteran status

- Household size

- Number of dependent children

- Insurance status of dependent children

- Employment

- Income (all sources)

- Release of information agreement

- Enrollment site

- Completion of Medicaid and PlusCare applications and status

- Completion of MIChild applications

Initially, these data were collected at the enrollment site and a paper record was submitted to the VODI central office. The central office then enrolled the patient, assigned a VODI number to the patient, and submitted the data to a clearinghouse, Health Decisions, Inc. Later, the registration process was completed by a Web-based system that verified the patient's lack of insurance and previous VODI enrollment. All VODI enrollees signed a consent form that allowed their personal health data to be shared with the VODI partners in order to create an enrollment and service database.

A Health Risk Appraisal was conducted on all enrollees. The appraisal captured whether the patient had diabetes, asthma, hypertension, cancer, tobacco use, or frequent emergency room use. Patients with these conditions were referred to the Disease Management Program (see Chapter 5). The patients who had at least one of the chronic health conditions listed above, were also asked to answer additional questions on the appraisal to further assess the immediacy of their need for help from the care or disease management programs.

Who Was Registered in VODI?

In all, 25,373 individuals were provided with coverage during the study period of December 1999 through December 2004. Of that group, 18,838 clients were enrolled in VODI, while the other 6,535 received public insurance as a result of VODI's assistance with the application process. The terms enrollee and clients are used interchangeably. VODI continues today to enroll those without health insurance, beyond the demonstration project time period and the Kellogg grant funding, which ended December 2004. VODI's current funding is a combination of VODI member dues assessments and grants. As of January 2007, VODI has found coverage for over 33,000 people who would have otherwise been without care.

Table 3.2 presents the demographic distribution of the 18,838 clients. Note that the VODI enrolled population was quite diverse. The highest percentages of VODI clients were African American, single, female, and employed (either part-time or full-time) and supported multiple family members.

Table 3.2. Characteristics of VODI Clients, 1999-2004 (n=18,838)

	Total VODI Clients Registered	
	Frequency	Percent
Gender		
Female	10,818	57.5
Male	7,994	42.5
Total	**18,812**	**100.0**
Age		
18-29 yrs	6,074	32.2
30-44 yrs	7,188	38.2
45-64 yrs	5,576	29.6
Total	**18,838**	**100.0**
Marital status		
Divorced	1,757	9.3
Married	2,756	14.7
Separated	864	4.6
Single	12,895	68.6
Widowed	537	2.9
Total	**18,809**	**100.0**
Ethnicity		
Arab American	58	0.3
Asian American	107	0.6
Black	16,627	92.4
Hispanic	493	2.7
Multiracial	4	0.0
Native American/Indian	40	0.2
Other	150	0.8
White	525	2.9
Total	**18,004**	**100.0**
Total monthly household income		
$0-$500	4,580	24.4
$501-$1,000	7,423	39.5
$1,001 or more	6,794	36.1
Total	**18,797**	**100.0**
Hours worked per week		
Unemployed	8,158	43.3
30 hours or less	2,774	14.7
30 hours or more	7,904	42.0
Total	**18,836**	**100.0**
Number in household		
1 person	4,213	22.4
2 people	4,758	25.3
3 or more people	9,857	52.4
Total	**18,828**	**100.0**
Chronic condition		
Yes	3,926	35.4
No	7,151	64.6
Total	**11,077**	**100.0**

VODI succeeded in reaching its target population: the low-income, working uninsured. A majority (56.7%) of VODI enrollees was employed and 43% reported working more than 30 hours a week. A closer look revealed more than half of those employed earned less than $8 hour. Working full time, this wage translates into an annual income of $16,640 per year. As most enrollees were supporting a family of at least three on this income, the average VODI client was near the 2004 federal poverty level ($15,670 for a family of three). To rise to 200% of the federal poverty level, a family of three would need to be supported by a full-time job at an hourly rate of more than $15. Only 20 percent of VODI enrollees (employed and unemployed) earned more than $8 per hour.

Because the enrolled population consisted of residents of Detroit, who were poor, unemployed, and African-American, demographic differences were evident when the VODI population was compared to national uninsured samples. According to 2004 data from U.S. Census Bureau, 57% of the uninsured in the United States are full-time workers, 16% works part time, and 27% are unemployed. A 2006 report from the Commonwealth Fund estimates that 64% of the uninsured are employed. Among VODI enrollees, 57% were employed; of those, nearly 15% worked part-time and 42% worked more than 30 hours per week. Nationally, 16% of the uninsured are African American, whereas in the VODI population, more than 92% were African American. The VODI population underrepresented Hispanics, who make up about one-third of the nation's uninsured population but composed less than 5% of VODI enrollees.[4]

The VODI enrollment and demonstration provides a glimpse into changes in the economic status of Detroit's uninsured since the beginning of the 21st century. The continuing decline in employer-based health insurance is an indication that increasingly more employed people will be uninsured. On the other hand, the loss of manufacturing jobs in Michigan (discussed in Chapter 1) has resulted in more unemployed people without health insurance. Additionally, the reduction in public insurance access from financial caps on the number that are covered can be expected to increase the number of employed, especially part-time workers without health insurance. A Robert Wood Johnson Foundation report uses survey data to show that 138,000 people in Michigan lost private-sector health insurance coverage between 1998 and 2003.[5] This is partly attributable to rising health insurance premiums paid by both employers and employees. The analysis

---

4.   Collins et al., *Filling Gaps in Health Insurance.*
5.   State Health Access Data Assistance Center, University of Minnesota, "Shifting Ground: Changes in Employer-Sponsored Health Insurance," May 2006, http://covertheuninsured.org/media/research/ ShiftingGround0506.pdf.

shows that in Michigan, the percentage of private-sector employees eligible for health insurance declined by 4%,[6] and the percentage that chose to enroll also fell 4.2% from 1998 to 2003.[7]

The data in Tables 3.3 and 3.4 further illuminate this issue. Table 3.3 shows the number of VODI enrollees over time by employment status at the time of enrollment. Table 3.4 reports the percentage of full- and part-time workers in the VODI database from 2000 to 2004.

Table 3.3. Employment Status of VODI Clients, 2000-2004

Employed	All Enrollment Sites											
	2000		2001		2002		2003		2004		2000-2004	
	#	%	#	%	#	%	#	%	#	%	#	%
No	334	26.1	550	22.0	3,129	44.0	1,997	44.3	1,162	35.1	7,172	38.3
Yes	944	73.9	1,955	78.0	3,976	56.0	2,515	55.7	2,151	64.9	11,541	61.7
All	1,278	100.0	2,505	100.0	7,105	100.0	4,512	100.0	3,313	100.0	18,713	100.0

The decline of employer-based coverage and the closure of PlusCare had a dramatic impact on the insurance status of VODI enrollees. Table 3.3 shows that the percentage of VODI enrollees who were unemployed doubled from 2001 to 2002. As the public insurance system was restricted and the unemployment rate in Detroit increased with the loss of manufacturing positions, more unemployed people sought to be enrolled in VODI. During the same period, the percentage of part-time workers grew from 40% to 63%. The lack of a publicly supported insurance program had a large impact on both unemployed and part-time employees. Most part-time workers are not eligible for health insurance from their employers. Table 3.4 confirms a continuing trend of more uninsured part-time workers, for whom employers typically limit benefits. These results are consistent with the decline in employer coverage reported by the Robert Wood Johnson Foundation.[8]

---

6.   Ibid, 17.
7.   Ibid, 21.
8.   Ibid.

Table 3.4. Percentage of VODI Clients Working More or Less Than 30 Hours per Week, 2000-2004

Hours Worked per Week	2000		2001		2002		2003		2004	
	#	%	#	%	#	%	#	%	#	%
30 hours or less	558	43.6	1,001	39.9	4,452	62.6	2,888	64.0	2,022	59.3
30 hours or more	721	56.4	1,509	60.1	2,655	37.4	1,626	36.0	1,388	40.7
All	1279	100.0	2,510	100.0	7,107	100.0	4,514	100.0	3,410	100.0

The financial resources of VODI clients clearly declined from 2000 to 2004. More people enrolled in VODI in 2004 worked fewer hours and at wages nearer the federal poverty line than those enrolled in 2000. Table 3.5 shows incomes declining from 2000 to 2003, a finding that is likely tied to the lack of public insurance programs. As the public insurance programs restricted new enrollees, poorer people turned to VODI as their health care safety net.

Table 3.5. Average Annual Income for VODI Enrollees, 2000-2004

Year	Average Annual Income
2000	$11,336
2001	$12,735
2002	$9,322
2003	$9,759
2004	$11,101

How Were the Services Provided to Enrollees Tracked?

Twelve health care sites provided VODI with service data on clients enrolled in the program. Table 3.6 shows each participating site and the time period for which it provided data. Variation in reporting was related to entrance of the sites into the program.

Table 3.6.: Time Period in Which Health Care Sites Provided Service Data, 1999: Q4-2004: Q4

Year	'99	2000				2001				2002				2003				2004			
Quarter	4	1	2	3	4	1	2	3	4	1	2	3	4	1	2	3	4	1	2	3	4
Health care site																					
Community Health and Social Services Midtown						▓	▓	▓	▓	▓	▓	▓	▓	▓	▓	▓	▓	▓	▓	▓	▓
St. John Community Health Center			▓	▓	▓	▓	▓	▓	▓	▓	▓	▓	▓	▓	▓	▓	▓	▓	▓	▓	▓
Detroit Community Health Connection	▓	▓	▓	▓	▓	▓	▓	▓	▓	▓	▓	▓	▓	▓	▓	▓	▓	▓	▓	▓	▓
Herman Kiefer (Detroit Health Department)	▓	▓	▓	▓	▓	▓	▓	▓	▓	▓	▓	▓	▓	▓	▓	▓	▓	▓	▓	▓	▓
Northeast Health Center (Detroit Health Department)	▓	▓	▓	▓	▓	▓	▓	▓	▓	▓	▓	▓	▓	▓	▓	▓	▓	▓	▓	▓	▓
Detroit Medical Center	▓	▓	▓	▓	▓	▓	▓	▓	▓	▓	▓	▓	▓	▓	▓	▓	▓	▓	▓	▓	▓
Health Centers Detroit		▓	▓	▓	▓	▓	▓	▓	▓	▓	▓	▓	▓	▓	▓	▓	▓	▓	▓	▓	▓
Henry Ford Health System		▓	▓	▓	▓	▓	▓	▓	▓	▓	▓	▓	▓	▓	▓	▓	▓	▓	▓	▓	▓
Mercy Primary Care						▓	▓	▓	▓	▓	▓	▓	▓	▓	▓	▓	▓	▓	▓	▓	▓
St. John Detroit Riverview -Emergency Room		▓	▓	▓	▓	▓	▓	▓	▓	▓	▓	▓	▓	▓	▓	▓	▓	▓	▓	▓	▓
St. John Hospital-Emergency Room			▓	▓	▓	▓	▓	▓	▓	▓	▓	▓	▓	▓	▓	▓	▓	▓	▓	▓	▓
Thea Bowman														▓	▓	▓	▓	▓	▓	▓	▓

Each site was allowed to submit data set in a format that was compatible with their existing billing or information system. The data from each site were submitted to the data clearinghouse. Each VODI partner was responsible for abstracting enrollee utilization data on primary care, emergency room use, specialty care, and inpatient care provided within its health system. In addition, admission date, discharge date, discharge status, and DRG (diagnosis-related groupings) codes were collected for inpatient stays. These data were harvested from each provider's quarterly reports for aggregation into the main VODI service database. The enrollment and claims data reported to VODI by participating providers were maintained in a manner compliant with all HIPAA (Health Insurance Portability and Accountability Act) reporting, privacy, and security requirements.

To ensure that consistent information was collected in the variable fields, a minimum data set for reporting was established. The following information was collected for each VODI client:

- **VODI number:** A unique VODI generated number was assigned to each VODI enrollee as a patient identifier that was used to track service utilization.

- **Service date**: The date of the patient's care encounter at the health care sites.

- **Service or patient type:** Allowed identification of the type of care received at each health care site. The main types of care included emergency room visits (ER), inpatient visits (IP), labs (LB), primary care visits (PC), and specialty care visits (SC). Each site used its own set of codes for this field, but a dictionary of codes was provided to the data clearinghouse and to VODI so that the information could be properly recoded.

- **Admit date:** Date of admission for an inpatient hospitalization.

- **Discharge date:** Date of discharge from an inpatient hospitalization.

- **Diagnosis codes**: Up to 10 diagnosis codes could be provided per client encounter.

- **Procedure codes**: Up to 10 procedure codes could be provided per client encounter.

- **Data source**: Identified the health care system or site that provided the data.

- **MRN:** The medical record number for each client at the particular health care site.

- **Location**: Identified the health care site that provided the service to the client.

- **Disposition status**: Identified the status of the patient at the time of discharge from the health care site. This was used primarily for inpatient care.

By collecting this information, the services could be quantified by person, place, and time, as well as by the type of care provided. In addition, the data permitted analyses to be carried out at an individual level, such that the evaluation was not limited to aggregate comparisons.

Because all of the organizations listed in Table 3.6 were organized into three enrollment and service networks, care could be tracked across the continuum of care within each network. Each provider site was sent a list of their enrollees from VODI and was asked to send back any data on services provided during the specified time period. Table 3.6 confirms that all of the sites provided data on the variables just outlined.

Did VODI Provide Coverage for Enrollees?

VODI's registration process was intended to function as insurance coverage for enrollees. The Institute of Medicine study outlined the following criteria for health insurance coverage: "The performance of health insurance plans and programs in facilitating a regular and continuing care relationship for enrollees should be a key factor in the design of any health insurance coverage reform."[9] VODI sought to simulate insurance coverage through virtual insurance. VODI coverage was virtual in that there was no payment to the provider. The coverage was simply the commitment of each VODI partner to provide and /or arrange for needed services for its assigned VODI enrollees.

To assess how close VODI came to simulating insurance, it was important to measure whether enrollees used VODI services and at what rates. Overall utilization rates are a proxy for coverage. The VODI tracking database showed that 53.8% of the people enrolled in VODI received service within their assigned network after the initial (enrollment) visit.

The strength of the VODI database was evident in that it allowed tracking of services provided over time for individuals who had previously been identified as uninsured and whose care was not uniformly or systematically tracked. Most analysis for insured populations' utilization relies on calculations of services per member or services per member month. Determining the denominator for these calculations in an uninsured population is difficult. The methodological issue is to determine the probability that an enrollee will use services at a given point in time. This was a limitation of the VODI data collection system. Because enrollees did not alert VODI when their status changed—that is, when they moved, died, or became insured—knowing precisely who was a member and who was

---

9.   Committee on the Consequences of Uninsurance, *Care without Coverage: Too Little, Too Late.* (Washington, DC: National Academy Press., 2002), 99.

not a member at any given time would have been particularly complicated. A methodology using services per VODI enrollee would understate the per member service utilization rate because it would include enrollees who had effectively left the program. Using only utilizers would have the opposite problem—it would overstate utilization rates compared to an insured population. This difference is illustrated in Table 3.7, which compares use rates for enrollees and utilizers over time.

Table 3.7. Use Rates for VODI Enrollees and Utilizers, 2000-2004

Year	Annual Enrollees	Cumulative Enrollees	Annual Utilizers	Annual Encounters	Encounters per Utilizer	Encounters/ Cumulative Enrollees
2000	1,279	1,279	468	1,475	3.15	1.15
2001	2,510	3,789	1,291	4,342	3.36	1.15
2002	7,107	10,896	3,404	11,114	3.26	1.02
2003	4,514	15,410	5,825	19,965	3.43	1.30
2004	3,412	18,822	5,176	17,756	3.43	0.94
Total	18,822	18,822	10,143	54,652		

Although Table 3.7 provides information on the encounters and services provided to VODI enrollees, the use rates in the last two columns are not comparable because the ratio of enrollees to utilizers changed. The cumulative enrollee column in Table 3.7 includes people who were no longer active. The drop in encounters per enrollee is magnified by the departure of people enrolled earlier in the program.

The lack of comparability is attributable to two factors. First, there is no accurate estimate of when an enrollee left the VODI program. One way to correct for this problem is to examine only those who used services. If an enrollee used services, then it is a good assumption that they were still participating in the program.

The second problem is that the time intervals for follow-up were not equal for all enrollees. The time available to use services was relative to the when an individual was enrolled. The probability that a 2002 enrollee used services is much greater than the probability that a 2004 enrollee used services. For example, clients enrolled after July 1, 2004, had only six months or less to return to a health care site following their enrollment, as service data were only available through the end of 2004. While newer enrollees may have needed to utilize services more heavily during their initial involvement with the program because of "pent-up need," our data show that some enrollees did not use services until six months or more after their enrollment date.

These two methodological issues can be demonstrated by examining the 2004 use rate (table 3.7) of 0.94 visits per enrollee per year—dramatically lower than the use rates for previous years. This lower rate is likely attributable to earlier enrollees from 2002, for example, leaving the program and no longer utilizing the services in 2004. Also, some of the enrollees from late 2004 may not have needed to acquire additional care yet.

One methodology for determining a denominator would restrict the analysis to only the utilizers of service. Service time intervals could then be calculated by using the time between the initial contact and subsequent visits as the active membership interval. However, different lengths of time for follow-up may still be a problem. While some researchers have addressed this problem by annualizing the rates, this seems like a risky methodology for those with a short length of time available for follow-up.[10] For example, if a client made two visits during their three months of available follow-up, then the annualized rate would be eight visits per year. One way to correct for this issue is to weight the annualized rates by the length of available follow-up time or to include a covariate that has the length of program participation.

Another approach is to use a set, specified post enrollment time interval during which the clients are still assumed to be participating and/or have equal opportunity to use services. In this case, a set, specified interval from the time of enrollment is examined, such that time frames with equal lengths but differing start and stop dates depending on the date of enrollment are created. The length of this time frame may be determined, as we did, by reviewing the literature and by examining the use rates of clients longitudinally.

Timothy McBride has determined the average length of time that uninsured individuals lack health insurance coverage. His analysis revealed that for non-poor uninsured people, the lack of coverage lasts an average of six months. The mean for low-income individuals is considerably longer, lasting an average of 8.3 months.[11] With this in mind, VODI decided to calculate use rates with only the service data within a one-year or twelve month post enrollment time frame. Given the variation in enrollment dates

---

10.   P. Diehr, D. Yanez, A. Ash, M. Hornbrook, and D. Y. Lin, "Methods for Analyzing Health Care Utilization and Costs," *Annual Review of Public Health* 20 (May 1999): 125–44.

11.   Timothy D. McBride, "Uninsured Spells for the Poor: Prevalence and Duration," *Health Care Financing Review* 19, no. 1 (1997): 145–60.

this will be a moving twelve month time frame calculated beginning with a person's enrollment date.

Taylor's examination of three "Communities in Charge" programs used categories of enrollees that were active after six months and enrollees active after 12 months.[12] VODI used similar enrollment categories based on the time frame of service utilization subsequent to enrollment. Categories were calculated for all service data from 1999 to 2004. Four coverage categories were created:

1. **None:** The enrollee did not use services subsequent to the enrollment visit.

2. **Early:** The enrollee used services only within six months of enrollment.

3. **Late:** The enrollee used services only after six months of enrollment.

4. **Continuous:**The enrollee used services within six months and after six months of enrollment.

This classification captures the extent to which enrollees were provided services by the enrollee's network. Enrollees in the early category used VODI coverage for less than six months, whereas the continuous category enrollees used VODI coverage consistently during the program.

Table 3.8. VODI Coverage Categories for Registered Participants, 1999-2003

Coverage Category	None		Early		Late		Continuous		Total	
	Number	%	Number	%	Number	%	Number	%	Number	%
Total	6,836	44.3	2,089	13.5	3,124	20.3	3,372	21.9	15,421	100.0

Table 3.8 shows that nearly 45% of enrollees did not use services and an additional 14% used services only in the first six months after registration. This table provides a stark reminder of how difficult it can be to engage those without health insurance. VODI's assurance that enrollees would receive care—at little or no cost to the patient—was an insufficient incentive

---

12.   Taylor et al., "Who Enrolls in Community-Based Programs for the Uninsured, and Why Do They Stay?" Exhibit 4.

to engage more than half of the enrollees (57.8%) after enrollment or beyond the first 6 months.

The categorization of enrollees into Early, Late and Continuous coverage patterns does not solve the problem of later enrollees having less chance to be in the service database. As noted above, the 2004 enrollees would by definition have less than 12 months of service data available in the service database. To correct this problem each enrollee's utilization is calculated on services provided in the first 12 months after registration and the analysis is restricted to those that have a full year's worth of data. Consequently, utilization can only be calculated on 15,421 people registered from 1999-2003. This provides all VODI enrollees with an equal probability of being in the VODI service database and allows calculation of use rates for active and inactive enrollees.

Figure 3.3 illustrates the number of active and inactive enrollees and shows the number of active enrollees who did and did not use services during the first 12 months after enrollment. The overwhelming majority of active enrollees (78%) used services in the first twelve months after enrollment.

Figure 3.3 Number of Active and Inactive Enrollees who Used Services during the first 12 months post enrollment.

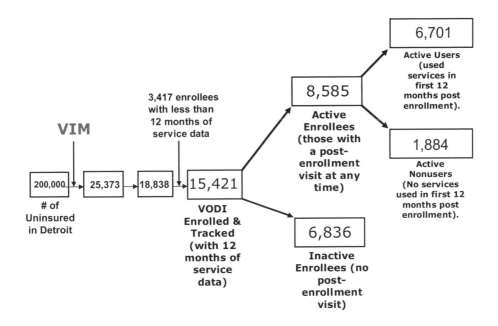

According to the figure, VODI active enrollees consisted of both users and nonusers, and therefore the sample is comparable to an enrolled insured population.

What Were the Characteristics of the Uninsured Who Used VODI Coverage?

A central question for any program for the uninsured is who needs and uses services. Safety net providers are likely to portray the uninsured as very sick and in great need of a wide variety of health care services. This characterization is attributable to the kinds of patients that safety net providers see, either in primary care settings or emergency rooms. However, this picture describes uninsured patients and does not consider uninsured nonpatients. An accurate picture of the uninsured requires that we combine users and nonusers. To outline strategies that will more successfully engage uninsured people in health care, it is important to know which client characteristics predict coverage use.

Logistic regression addresses this issue. Three alternative views were tested. One view is that health status, such as the existence of chronic conditions, leads to coverage use. Another view is that financial resources and economic barriers to coverage use are extremely powerful and difficult to overcome. The third view is that a person's historical health services utilization pattern influences subsequent coverage use. Logistic regression was used to understand these scenarios. Logistic regression shows the impact of each variable as a predictor of coverage category (active or inactive enrollee status) while controlling for the effect of all other variables in the model. The adjusted odds ratio shows the difference between the referent group and the variable category (the statistical techniques employed here are elaborated in Appendix B). Logistic regressions can be used to determine whether demographic, economic, or health factors are the most powerful in predicting post-enrollment use patterns. Table 3.9 presents the logistic regression for active and inactive VODI enrollees.

Table 3.9. Characteristics and Outcomes of Active and Inactive Enrollees

	Crude Odds Ratio		Adjusted Odds Ratio		Estimated Relative Risk	
	OR	95% CI	OR	95% CI	OR	95% CI
Enrollment location						
Emergency room	**0.82**	**0.74-0.91**	0.98	0.88-1.09	0.99	0.95-1.0
Other	**0.18**	**0.15-0.22**	0.21	0.21-0.26	0.41	0.35-0.47
Primary care	referent		referent		referent	
Gender						
Female	**1.67**	**1.53-1.82**	**1.57**	**1.44-1.73**	**1.24**	**1.20-1.29**
Male	referent		referent		referent	
Age						
18-29	referent		referent		referent	
30-44	1.01	0.29-1.12	0.97	0.87-1.08	0.99	0.93-1.04
45-64	**1.41**	**1.26-1.57**	**1.22**	**1.07-1.39**	**1.10**	**1.03-1.16**
Marital status						
Not married	referent		referent		referent	
Married	**1.19**	**1.08-1.30**	1.03	0.92-1.59	1.01	0.96-1.07
Total monthly household income						
$0-$500	referent		referent		referent	
$501-$1,000	**1.56**	**1.39.-1.75**	**1.24**	**1.09-1.41**	**1.12**	**1.05-1.19**
$1,001 or more	**1.48**	**1.32-1.66**	**1.16**	**1.01-1.34**	**1.08**	**1.01-1.16**
Hours worked per week						
Unemployed	referent		referent		referent	
30 hours or less	**1.32**	**1.15-1.50**	**1.30**	**1.12-1.50**	**1.13**	**1.06-1.20**
30 hours or more	**1.29**	**1.17-1.41**	**1.26**	**1.13-1.41**	**1.12**	**1.06-1.17**
Number in household						
1 person	referent		referent		referent	
2 people	1.14	1.00-1.29	1.10	0.96-1.26	1.05	0.98-1.11
3 or more people	1.02	0.92-1.15	1.04	0.92-1.17	1.02	0.96-1.07
Chronic condition						
Yes	**1.75**	**1.60-1.92**	**1.61**	**1.46-1.78**	**1.24**	**1.19-1.29**
No	referent		referent		referent	

The results in Table 3.9 indicate that, surprisingly, many demographic characteristics (number in household, age, marital status) did not have a powerful association with active enrollment. Gender, the existence of chronic conditions, income, and employment status all had a modest association with active enrollment. Thus, both health factors, such as the existence of a chronic condition, and financial resources, such as income and employment status, are moderate forces in determining whether the uninsured use care when coverage is provided. Lack of income and lack of employment are barriers to using health care coverage. The existence of chronic conditions is a motivator to use coverage. In this sample, people with chronic conditions were roughly 25% more likely to be active enrollees.

Emergency room enrollees and primary care enrollees were equally likely to become active. Thus, how a person sought health care did not seem to influence the probability of becoming an active enrollee.

Financial resources factors such as employment and income had an influence on post enrollment activity. Employed people were nearly 15% more likely to be active enrollees. Income also seems to have had an influence on post-enrollment use patterns. Enrollees who had some income were roughly 10% more likely to be active.

Conclusions

The organization and integration of coverage for the VODI uninsured provided useful information about that population. It also enabled enrollment workers to determine eligibility for public insurance coverage for a significant number of individuals who were screened. The enrollment and tracking system provided information that demonstrated that enrolled uninsured could be tracked and analyzed as if they had insurance.

The existence of chronic conditions provided motivation to seek care for those without health insurance, just as it does for those with insurance. Furthermore, the lack of economic resources is an obstacle to using coverage. The skills necessary to get and keep a job are the same as those needed to use health coverage. Being on time and keeping appointments are as important in health care as they are in employment. Having resources associated with full-time employment also allows a person to overcome economic barriers, such as the cost of transportation and child care.

Lessons Learned

Lesson 1: A significant benefit from screening the uninsured is the identification of people who are eligible for insurance.

Coordinating public and private insurance information
is essential to reduce the number of uninsured.

Lesson 2: Collaboration and coordination make it possible to build an
information system that can identify, track, and monitor care
for the uninsured. Such an information system is the foundation
for successful and supportive community interventions
to mange the care of those without health insurance.

Lesson 3: The organization of coverage and care must be
coordinated. Simply providing a coverage mechanism
without organizing a delivery system at the local level
will not ensure that uninsured individuals get the care
they need or that unnecessary costs are controlled.

Insurance coverage is critical but not sufficient for access
and appropriate service utilization. The mere existence
of coverage does not necessarily ensure access to care or
guarantee that care will be used appropriately. Furthermore,
the existence of safety net services does not necessarily
mean that services will be used or used appropriately.

Lesson 4: National and state reforms are implemented at the
community level. Therefore, community-driven solutions
are imperative if reforms are to be successful.

4

Care: Organizing the Delivery System

Figure 4.1. VODI Intervention Model (VIM): 4Cs

— Organize Collaboration
  - SJHS/HFHS/DMC/OHS/DHD/WCHD/WSU/FQHC
  - The framework for partnership of commitment, cooperation and agreement

— Organize Coordination
  - The act of working together in a common effort developing a common set of services and activities

— Organize Coverage
  - Registration
  - Enrollment
  - Medical Home Assignment
  - Tracking
  - Data Collection and Analysis

•Medical Home Use
•Preventive
•Primary Care

— Organize **Care**
  - **Medical Home Use**
  - **Basic Services:**
    - PC/Pharmacy/Lab/Dental
  - **Care Management**
  - **Disease Management**
  - **Subspecialty Care**
  - **Hospitalization**

↑**PC** ↓**ER** ↓**SC/Inpatient**

PC=Primary Care; ER=Emergency Room; SC=Specialty/Ancill/DiagCare

The fourth component of the Voices of Detroit Initiative (VODI) Intervention Model required an organized delivery system to provide care (Figure 4.1). Cunningham and Kemper[1] found that the ability of the uninsured to access needed medical care is subject to variation in the way that safety net services are organized and delivered. This chapter describes the delivery system and health care utilization patterns of VODI enrollees, with particular attention

---

1.   P. J. Cunningham and P. Kemper, "Ability to Obtain Medical Care for the Uninsured: How Much Does It Vary Across Communities?" *Journal of the American Medical Association* 280, no. 10 (1998): 921–27.

to primary care and emergency room visits. It also discusses identified service gaps in the safety net continuum of care and variation in how these were addressed in the VODI care networks. The service data collected for program enrollees is analyzed and discussed in this chapter. Lessons learned through the VODI Intervention Model, including benefits of the model for enrollees and participating providers, are outlined.

Several questions are explored here using the program data collected from participating providers during the five years of the program.

1. Did VODI enrollees have access to the full continuum of care?

2. Was the use of services consistent with the outcome goals of the VODI model? That is, did it increase primary care use, decrease emergency room use, reduce inpatient and specialty care, and transition patients from emergency to primary care?

3. Did the VODI model produce costs savings?

4. Which enrollee characteristics were associated with the outcome goals?

These and other questions are examined in this chapter using statistical analyses. Before outlining the findings, the context for this discussion will be set by describing the care model and the unique delivery system developed to care for program enrollees.

Background: The VODI Organized Delivery System

Through the process of collaboration and coordination, the three major hospital systems in the city, along with their partner safety net primary care centers, agreed to provide care to a defined number of VODI enrollees. The implementation and execution of the VODI Intervention Model established three organized networks of providers to care for assigned enrollees. Upon enrollment, each individual was assigned to a primary care medical home that served as the portal of entry into a full range of medical services, including basic preventive medical services, specialty services, and other hospital-based care. The focus and center of this organized delivery system of care was the primary care medical home.

The Federal Bureau of Primary Health Care defines primary care as "the provision of integrated accessible health care services by clinicians who are accountable for addressing a large majority of personal health care needs, developing a sustained partnership with patients, and practicing in the context of family and community."[2] This definition is consistent with the American College of Physicians' definition of a medical home that is detailed in Chapter 2. The important concept is that the primary care medical home is more than just a building or a place of care; it is also an approach to the provision of care.

Primary care is designed to be the first point of contact between an individual and the health care system. The ability to see a physician or other health care provider when one believes medical attention is needed is a fundamental aspect of access to care. Having a regular source of care improves the utilization of ambulatory care services, encourages the receipt of preventative services and the management of chronic conditions, and reduces emergency room visits and preventable hospitalizations. Adults without health insurance are more likely than those with insurance to lack a regular source of care.[3] In the VODI project, the medical home assignment ensured that each enrollee would have access to a regular source of care that would also manage each case as needed.

At the beginning of the VODI program, safety net providers in Detroit were only loosely affiliated and did not provide an organized system of care. The Institute of Medicine defines safety net providers as those that serve a significant patient population that is uninsured or dependent on Medicaid. In Detroit, there is no public hospital or pubic funding mechanism to support safety net providers. Existing safety net providers included three Detroit-based Federally Qualified Health Center (FQHC) agencies, which operated a total of six health centers around the city. One of these served primarily the homeless population through one health center and a "roving team." The Detroit Health Department also operated three safety net primary care sites. Of these, one served only women and children, one center served only adults, and one served all age groups. There were also at least three volunteer-based, part-time free clinics serving Detroit residents. Two statewide organizations served as the mechanism for affiliation between two of these types of providers, the Michigan Primary Care Association for FQHCs, and the Michigan Association for Free Clinics. Health systems with Detroit-based hospitals acted as default safety net providers through their hospital emergency rooms, which, by law (Emergency Medical Treatment and Active Labor Act-EMTALA), are obligated to serve anyone coming through their doors regardless of insurance status or ability to pay.

---

2. U.S. Department of Health and Human Services, *Changing Lives, Changing Communities through Primary Care* (Bethesda, MD: Bureau of Primary Care, 2001).
3. Committee on the Consequences of Uninsurance, *Care without Coverage: Too Little, Too Late* (Washington, DC: National Academy Press, 2002).

Furthermore, for safety net health centers, access to the full continuum of care for uninsured patients was fragmented and often inaccessible. This is consistent with other reports that primary care providers experience difficulty arranging for referrals for specialty, ancillary diagnostic, and treatment services, and other care they do not directly provide to the uninsured.[4,5] A few of the safety net primary care sites had arrangements or partnerships with a hospital to obtain services for their patients. However, there was great variation in how this care was accessed and, for the most part, it was not organized, timely, or well coordinated. It was also very costly. Without the presence of a public hospital in Detroit, each of these entities experienced difficulty obtaining timely, coordinated access to other health services, especially hospital-based and subspecialty care.

In summary, the condition of the Detroit safety net at the beginning of the VODI project was characterized by fragmentation, inadequate capacity, and lack of access to the full continuum of health services prior to the implementation of the VODI Intervention Model. The existing infrastructure—or lack thereof—had to be modified in order to deliver on the following four VODI goals:

1. Increased access to and utilization of primary care

2. Reduced emergency room utilization

3. Reduced preventable hospitalizations and specialty care utilization

4. Management of patients with chronic conditions (see Chapter 5)

The ability to access care is affected by both individual and community resources, characteristics, and need. The VODI Intervention Model sought to address the following factors:

- Individual resources by providing coverage and care at no cost or on an ability-to-pay basis for those with low incomes

- Individual characteristics through community and facility-based outreach to educate and enroll those in need

- Individual needs through the social work services available to program enrollees, as well as through

---

4.   M. Gusmano, G. P. Fairbrother, and H. Park, "Exploring the Limits of the Safety Net: Community Health Centers and Case for the Uninsured," *Health Affairs* 21, no. 6 (November–December 2006): 188–94.

5.   Sofia M. Franco, Charlene K. Mitchell, and Rosalia M. Buzon, "Primary Care Physician Access and Gate Keeping: A Key to Reducing Emergency Department Use," *Clinical Pediatrics* 36, no. 2 (February 1997): 63–68.

care and disease management for prevalent primary
care treatable chronic conditions (see Chapter 5)

- Community resources by organizing the delivery
  system into defined networks with an emphasis
  on primary care access and utilization

Furthermore, the VODI project removed or greatly reduced many of the typical barriers to accessing timely and appropriate care. Significant barriers to care included the following:

Lack of awareness of available safety net resources.

Hadley and Cunningham[6] report that less than half the uninsured are aware of and use the safety net providers in their community. This study is consistent with the findings of the Center for Studying Health System Change,[7] whose survey data indicate that most uninsured do not know where to get affordable care. All VODI enrollees were not only assigned to a primary care medical home but also to a network. The VODI central administrative office, staff, and community-based enrollment workers were resources for information on how to get assistance to address medical and some nonmedical needs of enrollees.

Out-of-pocket cost of care.

The Kaiser Commission on Medicaid and the Uninsured[8] has reported that 47% of the uninsured delay seeking care because of prohibitive costs. In the VODI project, all primary care providers applied a sliding fee scale based on the federal poverty guidelines or applied fees that were consistent with their existing charity care policy. Most of the hospital-based care within the network followed the same policy. In a large number of cases, services were provided without charge to the enrollee.

Time and convenience cost of obtaining care.

It is often inconvenient and time-consuming to obtain primary care. Distance to a health center and the ability to get a timely appointment are two factors that affect utilization.[9] In addition, the lack of paid sick time in many low-

---

6. Jack Hadley and Peter Cunningham, "Availability of Safety Net Providers and Access to Care of Uninsured Persons," *Health Services Research Journal* 39, no. 5 (October 2004): 15–46.

7. Laurie E. Felland, Suzanne Felt-Lisk, and Megan McHugh, "Health Care Access for Low-Income People: Significant Safety Net Gaps Remain," Center for Studying Health System Change, Issue Brief No. 84, June 2004, http://www.hschange.com/CONTENT/682/.

8. Jack Hadley and John Holahan, "The Cost of Care for the Uninsured: What Do We Spend, Who Pays, and What Would Full Coverage Add to Medical Spending?" Kaiser Commission on Medicaid and the Uninsured, Issue Update, May 10, 2004, http://www.kff.org/uninsured/7084.cfm.

9. Hadley and Cunningham, "Availability of Safety Net Providers and Access to Care of Uninsured Persons."

paying jobs is a barrier to primary care services, which are typically available only during the day. All VODI safety net providers had some, albeit limited, evening access to primary care. Most was on an appointment basis with limited walk-in availability.

The consequences of being uninsured are summed up by Hadley,[10] who has analyzed the research of the previous 25 years. He concludes that the uninsured

- Use fewer preventative, screening, and therapeutic services

- Are sicker when diagnosed

- Have poorer health outcomes (higher mortality and disability rates)

- Have lower annual earnings because of poor health

Hadley makes a compelling case that increasing medical care utilization in an appropriate setting for the uninsured would improve their health status.

How the VODI Delivery System Was Organized

With the current state of affairs in mind, the VODI collaborative took on the task of organizing the delivery system. Implementation of the VODI Intervention Model laid the foundation not only for improved collaboration, coordination, and coverage but also for the organization of existing safety net providers into a care-focused delivery system that was consistent with the program's goals and resources and the needs of both the uninsured and the community. Organizing collaboration, coordination, and coverage resulted in the establishment of care delivery networks.

A network is defined as a collection of professionals, agencies, hospitals, primary care centers, and other organizations that partner to provide the full continuum of health care to an assigned population. Initially, coordination resulted in the establishment of a basic or core package of services, with emphasis on utilization of and access to care through the assigned primary care medical home. It was recognized that an ongoing relationship with a primary care provider or system of care is a "hallmark of quality care."[11] Over a relatively short period of time, the full continuum was addressed within each of the three networks in a manner that was consistent with

---

10.   Jack Hadley, "Sicker and Poorer—The Consequences of Being Uninsured: A Review of the Research on the Relationship between Health Insurance, Medical Care Use, Health, Work, and Income," *Medical Care Research and Review 60, no. 2* (Suppl. 2003): 3S–75S.

11.   Committee on the Consequences of Uninsurance, *Care without Coverage.*

the unique resources, providers, relationships of each provider, and each network offered the VODI-defined package of services.[12]

The core services, coverage eligibility, enrollment process, and data reporting and tracking were integrated horizontally and were consistent across the networks. Meanwhile, the care delivery networks were integrated vertically to facilitate access to the full continuum of care and to promote continuity of care within a given network. Figure 4.2 illustrates the intra and inter network integration. These networks established partnerships between hospitals and safety net providers—a vital factor in the successful achievement of the model outcomes.

Figure 4.2

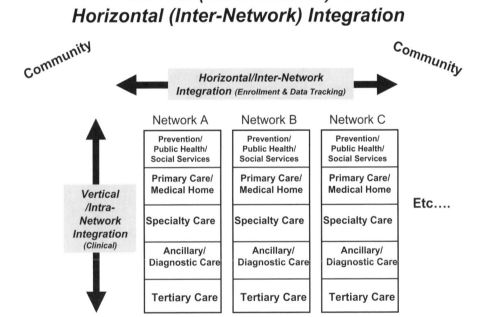

Vertical (Intra-Network) & Horizontal (Inter-Network) Integration

The hospital systems participated in the project voluntarily, even though there was no additional funding or mechanism to pay for the care rendered through these networks. The delivery system was organized around primary care medical homes, and each network included at least one hospital system. These networks and their arrangements for the continuum of care are outlined in Table 4.1.

---

12. Gusmano, Fairbrother, and Park, "Exploring the Limits of the Safety Net."

Table 4.1. VODI Care Networks by Service, 1999-2004

Service	Networks		
Primary care and care management	Detroit Community Health Connection (FQHC), private physicians, volunteer clinic	Community Heath and Social Services (FQHC), free clinic, Detroit Health Department Clinic	Advantage Health Centers (FQHC), Detroit Health Department, free clinic, volunteer clinic
Laboratory	Detroit Medical Center, Detroit Health Department	Henry Ford Health System, Detroit Health Department	St. John Health, Detroit Health Department
Pharmaceutical	Federally Qualified Health Centers, Detroit Health Department (Pharmaceutical Assistance Program)	Federally Qualified Health Center, Henry Ford Health System (Pharmaceutical Assistance Program), Detroit Health Department	St. John Health (Pharmaceutical Assistance Program), Detroit Health Department
Hospital-based diagnostics	Detroit Medical Center (Detroit Receiving Hospital)	Henry Ford Health System (Henry Ford Hospital)	St. John Health (Detroit Riverview Hospital, St. John Hospital)
Subspecialty care	Wayne State University Medical School	Henry Ford Health System	St. John Health Volunteer Physician Program
Inpatient care	Detroit Medical Center	Henry Ford Health System	St. John Health
Disease management	VODI Central Team	VODI Central Team	VODI Central Team
Emergency care	Detroit Medical Center (Detroit Receiving Hospital)	Henry Ford Health System (Henry Ford Hospital)	St. John Health (Detroit Riverview Hospital & St. John Hospital)
Dental	Referral to Detroit Health Department	Referral to Detroit Health Department	Referral to Detroit Health Department, Federally Qualified Health Center, or St. John Health Clinic

Note: Long-term care and rehabilitation services are not included in the VODI Intervention Model. Behavioral health services were provided through partnerships with the Detroit–Wayne County Mental Health Agency.

Types of Medical Homes

The networks included various types of safety net primary care providers who became the medical homes for enrollees. The five types are defined as follows:

1. **Federally Qualified Health Centers:** This is a community-based health center funded by the Federal Bureau of Primary Care, a division of the Health Resources and Services Administration. These facilities are also referred to as "PH330" clinics or centers. These sites have a mission to increase access to primary care for all, including both the insured and uninsured, in a medically underserved area. At the start of VODI project, there were three FQHCs in Detroit operating six health center sites. As a direct result of the VODI Intervention Model, Detroit's FQHC capacity was expanded to four organizations (Detroit Community Health Connection, Community Health and Social Services, Advantage Health Centers, and Health Centers Detroit Foundation, Inc.) operating thirteen health center sites.

2. **Local Health Department Health Centers:** The Detroit Health Department operates three primary care centers, two of which serve nonelderly adults in partnership with a health system at each site. Their mission is to serve as safety net primary care centers for the uninsured and Medicaid recipients.

3. **Volunteer clinics:** These are health centers that typically operate for less than 40 hours a week and have a mission to increase access to primary care for the uninsured and underserved. They may have one or two paid staff members, and the medical and clinical staff is composed primarily of volunteers. Acquiring and maintaining sustainable funding for supplies, rent, and so on is usually a great and ongoing challenge. Services are offered free of charge to patients. However, the scope of services provided may be very limited. The St. Vincent DePaul Health Center at Immaculate Heart of Mary Church, the Cabrini Clinic, and the Imani Health Center participated in the VODI project.

4. **Free Clinics:** Hospital and health systems, churches, and others frequently operate full-time (40 hours per week) safety net primary care health centers. Funding for these facilities is more stable and the scope of services provided more comprehensive. Services are

provided free to uninsured clients. St. John Community Health Center and Mercy Primary Care were project participants.

5.   **Employed/Private physicians:** Before gaining FQHC look-alike status, a network of nine health centers owned by Detroit Medical Center (DMC Health Centers Detroit) staffed by DMC employed physicians agreed to see a defined percentage of uninsured persons through VODI. In addition, Park Medical Centers designated one of its private practice health centers as a medical home for VODI patients in affiliation with the St. John Health System network. Henry Ford Medical Group family practice physicians provided services for VODI enrollees. St. John Health also employed physicians for services provided to VODI enrollees.

Types of Providers

The safety net primary care centers included clinical staff composed of physicians, nurse practitioners, and physician's assistants. In the state of Michigan, nurse practitioners may diagnose, prescribe, and treat medical conditions under the supervision of a physician. In several of the centers, nurse practitioners were the primary medical providers or clinicians. Patient satisfaction surveys indicate that patients are very satisfied with the level of care given by these providers.

Networks

The following is a brief description of the participating Detroit-based hospital systems. As indicated in Table 4.1, there was one hospital system in each network.

Detroit Medical Center

The Detroit Medical Center has provided excellent medical services in the metropolitan Detroit area since the founding of Children's Hospital in 1886. Detroit Medical Center/Wayne State University is the only academically integrated system in metropolitan Detroit and the largest health care provider in southeast Michigan. Detroit Medical Center has more than 2,000 licensed beds and 3,000 affiliated physicians, and it is the teaching, clinical, and research site for Wayne State University School of Medicine, the nation's fourth-largest medical school. The university's faculty and medical residents serve as the largest single provider of primary care to the underinsured and uninsured in the city of Detroit.

Only one of this system's eight hospitals, Detroit Receiving Hospital, participated fully in the VODI program, as this hospital handles the largest number of uninsured presenting to any facility in Detroit. Detroit Receiving Hospital is Michigan's first level-one trauma center and trains nearly 60% of Michigan's emergency department physicians. Detroit Medical Center's main safety net primary care partner is Detroit Community Health Connection (an FQHC), which operates five primary care centers.

At the beginning of the project, Detroit Medical Center had a network of nine primary care centers where it agreed to serve VODI uninsured enrollees. However, as a result of funding and organizational changes, the hospital system later divested itself of the nine health centers. Many of the physicians associated with these centers—with the help of the city, county, and state—applied and received an FQHC look-alike designation, operating as Health Centers Detroit Foundation, Inc. All of the VODI patients previously cared for at the nine DMC health centers were reassigned to Health Centers Detroit Foundation, Inc., and they continued to participate in the VODI program.

Henry Ford Health System

Henry Ford Health System is a nonprofit health system that provides more than 2.5 million patient contacts annually for residents in seven counties of southeast Michigan. It provides a comprehensive continuum of care with acute, specialty, primary, and preventive services backed by research and education. The system operates seven hospitals, 23 ambulatory medical centers, behavioral health services, and community care services, including pharmacies, dialysis centers, home care services, nursing homes, and hospice services. It is the home of the Henry Ford Medical Group, one of the nation's largest group practices, and Health Alliance Plan, a nonprofit managed care organization. Henry Ford Health System is affiliated with research and teaching programs at several prestigious universities. In addition, it is a nationally recognized health system with its main hospital in the center of Detroit. Community Health and Social Services, an FQHC, is its partner, operating three health centers. The system is also in partnership with the Detroit Health Department and provides the medical staff for one of its primary care centers, Herman Kiefer Health Center. During the course of the program, Community Health and Social Services received funding and opened a second primary care center in the city of Detroit.

St. John Health

St. John Health is a nonprofit, Catholic-sponsored health system that is one of the largest employers in metropolitan Detroit, with more than 18,000 employees. It provides comprehensive preventative, primary care, specialty, behavioral, long term care, home care, rehabilitation, cardiology, and cancer treatment and care with approximately 3,200 physicians, 125 medical offices, and seven hospitals spanning six counties in southeastern Michigan. It is the second highest provider of care to Medicaid recipients in the state of Michigan.

At the beginning of the VODI program, St. John Health operated three hospitals located on the east side of Detroit. Over the duration of the program, however, this system experienced many changes. As a result of major restructuring, St. John Health closed one hospital on the east side and added another across the city line on the west side of Detroit. Its safety net primary care centers include a nurse-managed center operated by the system; a Detroit Health Department site, Northeast Health Center, for which it provided medical staff; a volunteer-based, part-time health center located on the west side of Detroit; a site operated in partnership with Mercy Primary Care, a Catholic-sponsored safety net primary care provider; and Advantage Health Center, the remaining FQHC agency. During the course of the project, the FQHC was funded for and opened two other health centers. Geography was also an important factor in this network. Two St. John Health hospitals participated in VODI and paired with a medical home within the network. In addition, both hospitals were assigned a VODI enrollment worker for their emergency rooms.

Specialty Services

Hospital-based specialty care services were handled by arrangement within each network. The experience of the Detroit FQHC agencies has demonstrated that approximately 12% of those served in their health centers require specialty care referrals and other diagnostic or treatment services that are not available at the centers. There is no direct funding to pay for this type of care for the uninsured, creating a major access barrier and the possibility of less desirable health outcomes for people needing such care.

In this regard, there was no consistent approach to specialty services. Detroit Medical Center predominately relied on its partner, Wayne State University medical school faculty physicians to provide specialty services to its uninsured population. Henry Ford Health System provided specialty care for enrollees referred from its partner safety net sites through its employed medical staff. St. John Health developed a volunteer physician specialist network to provide care to its assigned population through a carefully structured program that closely monitored the number of patients sent to any one provider. A customized computer software program was developed for this purpose. At the time of this writing, more than 400 physicians were participating. Overall, VODI enrollees had access to needed specialty care. However, it must be noted that arrangements to provide many expensive specialty diagnostic procedures, such as MRIs or surgeries, continue to be fragile and at times challenging to obtain.

Pharmaceuticals

One particular and ongoing challenge is the area of pharmacy services. The steady rise in prescription drug expenditures is a serious problem for low-income and uninsured patients. While the cost-effectiveness of medication therapy is clear, the affordability of many medication treatment regimens is problematic. Patients with chronic conditions may be faced with insurmountable costs and may decide to reduce their doses, split tablets, use medication samples or foreign medications, substitute nonprescription products, or simply forgo drug therapy altogether, to the detriment of their health status and quality of life. To date, no single method of providing pharmaceuticals to VODI enrollees has been used by all safety net providers. The following strategies have been used to provide pharmaceuticals:

- **Detroit Health Department:** The department operates a pharmacy that fills prescriptions for Health Department clinic patients. A formulary is used that is consistent with its federal 340B status, other state discounts for specified drugs, and the department's budget. No narcotics or potentially addictive drugs are included in the formulary. Patients were not charged for the cost of the prescriptions during the demonstration phase of VODI. Prescriptions were filled for patients of selected safety net primary care centers without charge to the patients. However, because of increased demand and cost, a modest charge per prescription has since been instituted.

- **Federal 340B program:** Federally Qualified Health Centers have federal 340B designations for pharmaceuticals, which allow them to obtain most drugs at a substantial discount. Again, there was significant variation in implementation among the three FQHC agencies. One obtained drugs from the Detroit Health Department based on a long-standing relationship. One established a relationship with the Health Department to purchase drugs at a discounted price. The third agency developed an innovative relationship with a local pharmacy that was consistent with 340B regulations. Agencies are allowed to charge based on a sliding fee scale for these purchases.

- **Indigent drug programs:** Although somewhat complicated and time intensive, several sites hired and trained personnel to enroll their patients in the various pharmaceutical company indigent drug programs. One volunteer-based safety net health center estimated receiving an average of more than $500,000 annually in free medications for its clients. This strategy continues to expand as a method of obtaining

pharmaceuticals with innovative software and other programs
that facilitate access to and management of these programs.

Access to pharmaceuticals is of major importance in improving care
for patients with multiple chronic diseases. It is also very expensive. VODI
enrollees received an average of 10.54 prescriptions per year. To reduce
the financial burden, both the Detroit Health Department and St. John
Riverview Hospital, which provided pharmacy services to VODI patients,
took advantage of the Health Resources and Services Administration's
340(B) program to receive pharmaceuticals at a greatly reduced price. The
average national cost per prescription filled is roughly $57.00; through
Detroit Health Department/VODI program, however; the average cost was
approximately $12.12 per prescription. Prescription information for VODI
was submitted electronically on a regular basis to the VODI central office
by the pharmacies of the Detroit Health Department. This information was
linked to VODI registration data and analyzed by VODI staff to produce
aggregate numbers that may be shared across the health systems.

Dental Care

Dental care was identified early on as a major need and service gap. Oral health
services continue to be a challenge for VODI. Although one new dental clinic
was added at the Thea Bowman site, the Detroit Health Department program
still struggles with insufficient resources. Furthermore, St. John Community
Health Center faces funding issues related to dental care. Though a service
gap may still exist, some of the sites partnering with VODI have been able
to offer low-cost dental care. Detroit Community Health Connection and
Community Health and Social Services operate dental clinics, and the Thea
Bowman Center applied for additional funding to expand its dental services.
The new FQHC location, Advantage Family Health Center now has a plan
for a four-chair dental clinic. Detroit Community Health Connection's
Nolan Community Health Center site has four chairs that are not currently
staffed, and the Community Health and Social Services Midtown site has
unstaffed chairs. All of these programs expect to staff their dental clinics in
the near future.

Patient Fees

One of the significant known barriers to the receipt of primary care is the cost.
Studies have indicted that co-payments, patient fees, and other direct costs
to patients may be a barrier to seeking and receiving timely and appropriate
care. This is especially true for low-income individuals and families and for

patients with chronic diseases. The VODI partners agreed on two principles in this regard in the context of this demonstration project:

- The existing fee structures of the participating organizations would remain unaltered. An assessment of participating primary care providers indicated that all but one center was providing care free of charge or using a sliding fee scale (based on ability to pay and federal poverty guidelines) for enrollees. The one exception charged a flat fee of $20 for each primary care visit. This variation in fees was also applied to payments for pharmaceuticals. However, patients presenting to an emergency room may be subject to charge by any on-call private physician needed to provide care to these patients. They may receive a bill in this regard. Attempts to modify this situation for VODI enrollees were unsuccessful.

- Hospitalization was typically covered for those low-income enrollees eligible for Medicaid only after the application of the state "spend-down" guidelines. The participating hospitals each had a charity care policy that greatly discounted or eliminated any charge to patients for inpatient care.

Utilization Patterns of VODI Registrants

The organized delivery system in the VODI Intervention Model was designed to deliver care to uninsured people enrolled by VODI partners. The organized delivery system was expected to result in more optimal use of health care services, including the following outcomes:

- Continuum of care provided to uninsured clients

- Medical home utilization

- Transition from emergency to primary care

- Decreased emergency room use

Chapter 3 identified 8,585 registrants who accepted VODI coverage and utilized services after their initial enrollment visit. This group of people serves as the population for most of the analyses in this chapter. The rates of service use were calculated for the first 12 months following enrollment. This time frame allows each enrollee an equal probability of using services and addresses the problem of those who may have received coverage from another source, effectively "disenrolling" themselves from the program. The analyses in this chapter are limited, however, in that there are no data on the prior health care utilization patterns of VODI enrollees. Also, it is unknown whether any enrollees used services outside the VODI networks.

The following facts in conjunction with the methodology discussion in the chapter 3 section "Did VODI provide coverage for enrollees", will help readers understand the discussion in the remainder of this chapter, as outlined in Figure 4.3.

- A total of 18,838 uninsured people were enrolled in VODI over the duration of the demonstration phase, which ended December 31, 2004.

- In all, 15,421 (81%) VODI enrollees were tracked during the 12 months following enrollment. The remaining 3,417 (19%) enrollees participated in the program for less than 12 months because they were enrolled during the last year of the study period.

- Of those with at least 12 months of enrollment, 8,585 (56%) were active enrollees (they used services of any kind at any time after enrollment), and 6,836 (44%) were inactive enrollees (they used no services after enrollment).

- A total of 5,453 (63% of the active enrollees) used medical home services during their post-enrollment history, whereas 3,132 (37%) did not. However, the latter used other kinds of VODI services, such as dental, emergency room, specialty, or inpatient care.

- The initial enrollment visit is not included or counted as a visit in these analyses.

Figure 4.3. Active and Inactive Enrollees Who Used Services during the First Year after Enrollment

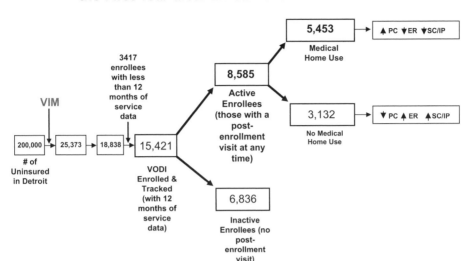

The analyses in this chapter are based on use rates among comparison groups of VODI active enrollees. The comparison groups were constructed based on the entire history of a person's VODI experience, although a possible limitation of this analysis is that earlier enrollees may have more service data. The comparison groups were constructed based on whether the enrollee's experience included the following:

- **Medical home use:** A comparison was made between enrollees who used the medical home and those who did not during their entire history with VODI. We would expect a lower rate of emergency room use for those who use the medical home compared to those who do not.

- **Transition from emergency room to primary care:** A total of 8,255 enrollees registered at participating emergency rooms had at least 12 months of enrollment. Of these, 4,584 used services. Those who made a primary care visit were compared to those who did not. We would expect that those who made a visit or transitioned to primary care would have lower rates of emergency room, specialty care, and hospitalization use than those who did not.

- **Frequent emergency room use:** This group includes those who made three or more emergency room visits per year during the length of their active participation in VODI compared to those who did not. Active participants were determined by comparing the last date of service to their enrollment date.

Question 1: Did VODI Enrollees Experience Access to the Full Continuum of Care?

The VODI core services were provided by each of the networks, and the care of each enrollee or utilizer was managed through his or her assigned primary care medical home. From 2000 to 2004, the three networks provided more than 70,000 visits or encounters to these registrants. Of these visits, 34% were for primary care, only 12% were for emergency room care, and 19% were for specialty care. Table 4.2 clearly demonstrates that a significant amount of service was rendered through the networks. In addition, the utilization of services occurred across the full continuum of care. The table does not include disease management utilization, which is discussed in Chapter 5.

Table 4.2. Visits Made by Active Enrollees Registered before January 1, 2004, for Service Period 1999-2004, (N = 8,585)

Type of Care Provided	Number of patients	Number of visits
Emergency care	3,686	8,829
Inpatient care	907	1,327
Primary care	5,448	24,166
Pharmacy*	2,862	21,595
Specialty care	2,884	14,217
Dental**	189	338
Total	*15,976****	*Total* 70,468*

* Includes data from the Herman Kiefer pharmacy and Northeast pharmacy for only a portion of the five-year project; therefore, pharmacy services are undercounted.

** Includes data from Herman Kiefer and Northeast for dental and laboratory visits for only a portion of the five-year project. This table includes a revised column for number of patients, as the table in Chapter 3 had clients enrolled through the end of 2004, whereas this analysis considers those enrolled before January 1, 2004.

*** This is not an unduplicated total, as patients may have used one or more types of care.

The data represent the number of visits or encounters. An individual enrollee may have had multiple visits in several of the categories over the duration of the period. An "encounter" occurred when an enrollee made a visit on any given day at a specific site. Changing locations within a facility is not counted as a separate encounter, although showing up at the same facility on two different days would be counted as two separate encounters. It is important to note that these figures represent the entire VODI care network, including not only hospitals but also the safety net primary care partners. For the most part, these services were provided without significant charge to the patient because the cost of care was supported by each of the network's providers.

It is unlikely that such an extent of specialty and other types of care would have been provided to these individuals in the absence of the VODI implementation model and the accompanying organized delivery system of care. In a report outlining the key findings of the 2003 National Health Interview Survey,[13] nearly half of all nonelderly adults (n = 25,093) reported having one or more chronic conditions. Additionally, the report stated that 38% of uninsured adults with a chronic condition reported forgoing needed medical care, and 34% reported an unmet need for prescription drugs. They also had difficulty obtaining other services, such as expensive diagnostic tests, and specialty care in a timely, well-coordinated fashion. The Institute of Medicine[14] has reported that "except for emergency room services, which are used comparably at about 11% by privately insured and uninsured persons, the proportion of the uninsured population using any other kind of health service is one half to two thirds of the proportion of the privately insured population using each type of service."[15]

Overall, the project succeeded at providing at least one full year of coverage and access to the continuum of services to 81% (N = 15,421) of enrollees after registration. By virtue of the enrollment process and medical home assignment, all 18,838 enrollees were linked to a primary care medical home, and 15,421 were enrolled and covered for at least 12 months. Baker et al.[16] found that those who are not continuously insured are more likely to have a major health decline than those who are continuously insured or covered. Those enrolled earlier in the program had one to three years of coverage. We were limited in our ability to statistically analyze whether the organized delivery system changed the utilization patterns of the uninsured because there are no data on utilization prior to enrollment in the program. However, the analyses in this chapter, the literature, and anecdotal evidence all suggest that VODI succeeded at transitioning enrollees to more optimal health-seeking and utilization behaviors, resulting in improved health outcomes.

---

13. Hadley and Cunningham, "Availability of Safety Net Providers and Access to Care for Uninsured Persons."
14. Committee on the Consequences of Uninsurance, *Hidden Costs: Value Lost* (Washington, DC: National Academy Press, 2003).
15. Ibid.
16. David W. Baker, Joseph J. Sudano, Jeffrey M. Albert, Elaine A. Borawski, and Avi Dor, "Lack of Health Insurance and Decline in Overall Health in Late Middle Age," *New England Journal of Medicine* 345, no. 15 (2001): 1106–12.

A 57-year-old African American male, single with four adult children, was employed full time as security guard. His employer did not offer health insurance, and he did not earn enough to pay for private health insurance. He became ill and unable to work in May 2005. He presented to one of the safety net centers with complaints of stomach pain and associated gastrointestinal (GI) bleeding, headache, and vision problems. He was enrolled into the VODI program. The physician diagnosed him with a bleeding ulcer and treated him, but in light of his progressive headaches and visual problems, the patient was subsequently referred to a partner hospital for an MRI of the brain. The MRI identified a pituitary tumor of the brain. He was able to see a gastroenterologist and neurosurgeon at that hospital for treatment. Subsequent surgery was performed to remove the pituitary tumor. After his discharge from the hospital, he was seen by an endocrinologist to further evaluate his pituitary function. Four months after his initial visit to the health center, he returned to work full time. Without the VODI delivery system, it is likely that his treatment would have been delayed, during which time his condition could have worsened, resulting in permanent physical damage, permanent loss of work, and financial hardship for himself and his family and creating preventable long-term costs for medical and social service support needs.

Question 2: Was the Use of Services Consistent with the Outcome Goals of the VODI Model?

In this section, utilization patterns are examined for primary care, emergency room, and inpatient and specialty care for enrollees. Note that reported specialty care was linked to inpatient hospitalization. Therefore, the two have been combined into one category for the purposes of this analysis. Another note is that the analysis in this chapter counts ER visits resulting in hospitalization in the category of inpatients visits. These visits are not also counted in the category of ER visits, which was limited to encounters where the patients were discharged from the ER. Tables 4.3–4.7 are discussed in this section.

Primary Care Utilization

Delving a bit deeper into the pattern of primary care utilization, we can look at the location where enrollees had their first visit subsequent to registration.

Table 4.3 indicates that for active enrollees ($n = 8,585$), about half (53.3%) went to the primary care site, only 27.0% went to the emergency room, and 18% sought inpatient or specialty on their first visit after enrollment. It is significant and noteworthy that 61.5%% of emergency room active enrollees ($n = 4,584$) did not have an ER visit with discharge for their first subsequent post-enrollment encounter. They, instead, went to their assigned primary care medical home (39.4%); required inpatient and or specialty care services (20.8%), or had some other type of health care utilization (0.3%).

Primary care active enrollees were much more likely to stay in primary care after enrollment. More than two-thirds (70.6%) of primary care active enrollees returned to primary care on their first visit after enrollment. Table 4.3 confirms that factors other than the medical home assignment may have a greater influence on the behavior and care-seeking patterns of uninsured individuals. This is good news for people who already have a primary care provider but bad news for those who are trying to transition from the emergency room to the primary care clinic. This finding is consistent with the work of Grumbach, Keane, and Bindman,[17] who found that emergency room use was lower for those with a regular source of care than those without. Primary care active enrollees are more likely to establish a regular source of care than those enrolled in the emergency room. Other researchers have suggested that the emergency room may be used as a main source of care because it is convenient. Other barriers may also hinder transition. Overall, about 60% of VODI active enrollees made 24,166 primary care visits from 1999 to the end of 2004. Furthermore, Table 4.4 indicates that of the emergency room active enrollees who went to their assigned primary care medical homes on their first visit after enrollment, 53.8% made a second or later visit to the primary care center. This indicates a change in utilization pattern: Primary care utilization increased and emergency room utilization decreased.

---

17.   K. Grumbach, D. Keane, and A. Bindman, "Primary Care and Public Emergency Department Use Overcrowding," *American Journal of Pubic Health* 63, no. 3 (March 1993): 372–78.

Table 4.3. Type of Visit on First Encounter after Enrollment for Clients with a History of Utilization after Enrollment (*N* = 8,585)

Group of enrollees examined	Type of Visit on First Encounter after Enrollment					
	Primary Care		Emergency Room		Inpatient or Specialty Care	
	Number	%	Number	%	Number	%
Active enrollees (those with subsequent utilization after enrollment (*N* = 8,585))	4,577	53.3	2,320	27.0	1,535	17.9
Active emergency room enrollees (those with subsequent utilization after enrollment (*N* = 4,584))	1,808	39.4	1,764	38.5	952	20.8
Active primary care enrollees (those with subsequent utilization after enrollment (*N* = 3,755))	2,650	70.6	464	12.4	553	14.7

Note: Clients were enrolled from the fourth quarter of 1999 to the fourth quarter of 2003. The total number of enrollees during this time period was 15,421, of which, 8,585 were active enrollees. A small percentage of clients could not be categorized as having received primary care, emergency room, or inpatient or specialty services on their first visit. (Row percents do not have total of 100% because the "other" category for visits and registration site is not shown here.)

Emergency Room Utilization

Of particular interest to hospital administrators are factors that influence emergency room utilization. Table 4.3 indicates that 39.4% of emergency room active enrollees made their first visit after enrollment to their primary care medical home, and 38.5% returned to the emergency room. Table 4.4 examines what happened on the second or later visits after registration for emergency room active enrollees. About 55% of the emergency room enrollees continued to return to the emergency room for additional care. By the same token, 15.0% of emergency room active enrollees who made their first visit after registration to the emergency room went to their primary care medical home on the second visit. This indicates a change in behavior, although it occurred a bit later after enrollment. Clients from the emergency room who got to the primary care medical home on the first visit after enrollment (53.8%) continued to seek care there on the second visit. Again, primary care increased, and emergency room utilization decreased.

Table 4.4. Service Use on Second and Later Visits by Emergency Room Active Enrollees (*N* = 4,584)

Active Emergency Room Enrollees	Type of Encounter on Second and Later Visits					
	Primary Care		Emergency Room		Inpatient/ Specialty Care	
	Number	%	Number	%	Number	%
First visit to emergency room (*N* = 1,764)	270	15.0	986	54.9	540	30.1
First visit to primary care medical home (*N* = 1,808)	1,081	53.8	488	24.3	439	21.93
First visit to inpatient/specialty care (*N* = 952)	166	14.7	336	29.7	628	55.6

Note: Clients were enrolled through the emergency room from the fourth quarter of 1999 to the fourth quarter of 2003. The total number of registrants from the emergency room for this time period was 8,255, with 4,585 who used services and had at least 12 months of data.

The most effective strategy for moving people from emergency to primary care requires ensuring a first visit to primary care. Caution is needed here, in that one limitation of this analysis is that the pre-intervention primary care utilization pattern of VODI registrants is unknown, as this data was not collected. Once the patient transitions to a medical home, they typically continue to use it. These data suggest that contacting and referring patients who present to the emergency room is an effective outreach strategy.

Inpatient and Specialty Care

These two categories are analyzed together because the data reported to VODI indicated that a majority of the reported specialty care was linked to inpatient hospitalization. Table 4.3 indicates that, overall, 17.9% percent of active enrollees made their first visit after enrollment for inpatient or specialty care, compared to 20.8% for emergency room active enrollees and 14.7% for primary care active enrollees. Those who continued to use the emergency room on their second visit had significantly higher inpatient or specialty care use (30.1%) than those who transitioned to primary care (21.9%). Emergency room active enrollees whose first visit was to inpatient or specialty care (55.6%) continued to show higher rates of inpatient or specialty care use (Table 4.4). It is likely that these enrollees were very sick individuals who required more intensive acute care. This is consistent with the finding that the uninsured tend to delay seeking care, which may worsen their condition. However, those who used primary care early on had a lower rate of hospitalization or specialty care utilization. The VODI Intervention Model performed as expected in this case.

Throughout the VODI program, there was a focus on moving the uninsured, particularly those with conditions that could be treated in a primary care setting, out of the emergency room and into lower-cost safety net primary care centers. This strategy is in keeping with the evidence that patients use the emergency room for nonemergency conditions because they lack knowledge of available alternatives for care or experience barriers (financial or other) to accessing care. There was successful transition to and utilization of primary care and other services after registration for about half of all VODI active enrollees. However, the question remains, did the use of the medical home reduce emergency room utilization. The short answer is yes. Consider the following.

Table 4.5 compares emergency room utilization for medical home users and nonusers after registration. It looks at the emergency room utilization pattern of active enrollees (those who used services and were enrolled for at least 12 months). Clearly, those who visited or transitioned to a primary care medical home had a significantly lower rate of emergency room utilization (31.0/100 enrollees) than those who did not (84.6/100 enrollees).

Table 4.5. Emergency Room Utilization for Medical Home Users versus Nonusers among Active Enrollees (N=8585)

	Cohort	Emergency Room Visits	Rate per 100 Enrollees
No medical home use	3,132	2,651	84.6
Medical home use	5,453	1,690	31.0

The VODI Intervention Model sought to reduce emergency room use, not necessarily to reduce the overall use of care by the uninsured. In fact, an incentive for participants to enroll in VODI was that the barriers to primary care would be greatly reduced. Examination of the cohort that successfully transitioned to a primary care medical home should show no decrease in overall utilization when compared to those who did not transition to a medical home. This is addressed in Table 4.6, which compares the overall use rates for enrollees who transitioned to a medical home to those who did not. Table 4.6 indicates that those who used their medical home had a significantly higher rate of utilization of *all* services (375.7/100 enrollees) compared to those who did not use their medical home (219.7/100 enrollees). Both observations are consistent with the VODI model in that the primary care medical home is the avenue for managing the patient care, including the facilitation of timely and coordinated access to other needed services. Table 4.6 also confirms that medical home users had a much lower rate of emergency room utilization than for those who did not use their medical home.

Table 4.6. Service Use among Active Enrollees Who Transitioned from Emergency Room Registration to Medical Home (*N* = 4,584)

	Cohort	Overall Use (per 100 enrollees)	Primary Care Use (per 100 enrollees)	Emergency Room Use (per 100 enrollees)
No successful medical home transition	2,379	219.7	0	97.2
Successful medical home transition	2,205	375.7	222.8	53.0

Note: Includes clients who were enrolled through the emergency room from the fourth quarter of 1999 to the fourth quarter of 2003 and had documented service utilization after registration. The determination of successful primary care assignment was made by examining a client's entire utilization history within the assigned VODI network after registration, whereas the utilization rates are based on service visits after registration within one year of the client's registration date.

These findings are consistent with the premise of the VODI Intervention Model that having a regular source of care influences behavior so as to increase primary care utilization, reduce emergency room utilization, and improve health outcomes. In table 4.7, those who used their medical home had a significantly lower emergency room utilization rate (31.0/100 enrollees) than those who did not use their medical home (84.6/100 enrollees). In short, having a regular source of care is a powerful predictor and influencer of access to primary care.[18] Conversely, frequent emergency room users had a significantly lower primary care rate (59.4/100 enrollees) and higher emergency room use rate (194.5/100 enrollees) than those who were not frequent emergency room users (table 4.7). Among emergency room enrollees who transitioned to primary care, the emergency room use rate was 53.0/100 enrollees. Those who did not transition had a rate of 97.2/100 enrollees. Clearly, then, medical home use reduces emergency room use for this population.

18. Cheryl Merzel and Joyce Moon-Howard, "Access to Health Services in an Urban Community," *Journal of Urban Health* 79, no. 2 (June 2002): 186–99.

Table 4.7 provides data that supports and reinforces other findings on health care utilization and clearly demonstrates the positive impact of the VODI intervention. Active enrollees who were successfully transitioned to a medical home from their initial emergency room registration point used more services (375.7/100 enrollees) than those who were not transitioned to a medical home (219.7/100 enrollees) (tables 4.6 & 4.7). Therefore, access to needed care was substantially improved. The cost implications of this finding are addressed later in this chapter.

Table 4.7. Overall Use Rates among Active VODI Enrollees (*N* = 8,585)

	Use Rate (per 100 enrollees)			
	Primary Care	Emergency Room	Other	Total
Medical home use Yes (*N* = 5,453) No (*N* = 3,132)	243.5 0	31.0 84.6	80.0 120.4	354.5 205.0
Frequent emergency room use Yes (*N* = 1,354) No (*N* = 7,231)	59.4 172.5	194.5 23.6	121.8 89.7	375.6 285.8
Transitioned to medical home from emergency room Yes (*N* = 2,205) No (*N* = 2,379)	222.8 0	53.0 97.2	99.9 122.5	375.7 219.7

> *One of the VODI participating health centers treated a 50-year-old male with rheumatoid arthritis who had been homebound for five years. He indicated that his arthritis had gotten out of control since he had lost his insurance years ago. He was barely able to walk because of inflammation in his knees and feet. Unable to work and unable to qualify for disability, he lived in his daughter's basement. His humiliation and frustration were almost as great as his pain. As a result of weekly visits to the health center, he was able to find the right medication regimen. He is now able to walk without great pain, can take short walks, and is able to baby-sit his grandchildren while his daughter works. He now has a new lease on life and maintains regular quarterly appointments at the health center. At every appointment, he thanks the health center staff for his greatly improved health.*

Question 3: Did the VODI Model Produce Costs Savings?

For health care policy makers and providers, especially safety net providers, a key question is, did the change in care utilization patterns described here reduce cost of care? The answer is yes. Increased medical home use, reduced emergency room use, and programs to transition emergency room patients to medical homes proved to be cost-saving strategies for struggling safety net providers and payers.

The dollar value of changing use patterns can be roughly approximated by considering cost estimates for primary care visits, emergency room visits, and inpatient/specialty visits. Because the VODI partners did not provide cost data as part of the minimal data set, we must estimate costs. One hospital partner estimated the total cost of care for their VODI enrollees. They reported a total annual average cost of $3,018 per patient. This cost included emergency room care but excluded services provided in primary care settings.

Medicare outpatient cost data were used to calculate primary care cost. The cost of a primary care visit was calculated by taking the value for primary care CPT-4 codes in the Medicare cost report and multiplying by the number of times the code occurred in the service database, then dividing by the number of VODI encounters. Using this approach, the value of a primary care visit or cost of care per visit was estimated at $78.30.

A study by Bamezai, Melnick, and Nawathe calculated the cost of an emergency room visit to be $412 for emergency rooms with a trauma center.[19] The estimate of "other costs" was calculated by subtracting $1,788,492, the total cost of emergency room encounters among patients ($412 x 4,341 encounters), from the total cost of care reported by the hospital ($13,080,012 = $3,018 x 4,334 patients) for non–primary care patients. Total other costs per visit were estimated at $1,359.53. This estimate was calculated by dividing $11,291,520 by the number of other visits (8,303).

Our cost calculations are consistent with other researchers. Hadley and Holahan estimated that the annual per capita cost of care for an uninsured person at $1,864 and the annual per capita cost of care for an insured person at $3,653.[20] Using the cost estimates above, the per patient costs for the VODI project were $2,107 annually. Our cost calculation is therefore consistent with Hadley and Holahan's cost estimate for the uninsured.

Table 4.8 uses above cost estimates to examine the cost savings of utilization change for each of the three comparison groups discussed earlier in this chapter. The use rate per 100 active enrollees is converted to a group cost per 100 active enrollees using the estimates for primary care, emergency room care and inpatient/specialty care. Savings per 100 active enrollees are calculated in the last column of Table 4.8.

Table 4.8. Cost Savings of the VODI Model

	Visits per 100 Active Enrollees per Year			Group Cost per 100 Active Enrollees per Year				VODI Savings per 100 Enrollees per Year
	Primary Care	Emergency Room	Other	Primary Care	Emergency Room	Other	Total	
Medical home use								$(57,942)
Yes (N = 5,338)	243.5	31	80	$19,066	$12,772	$108,762	$140,600	
No (N = 3,466)	0	84.6	120.4	0	$34,855	$163,687	$198,543	
Frequent emergency room use								$(105,196)
Yes (N = 1,354)	59.4	194.5	121.8	$4,651	$80,134	$165,591	$250,376	
No (N = 7,231)	172.5	23.6	89.7	$13,507	$9,723	$121,950	$145,180	
Medical home transition								$(31,491)
Yes (N = 2,092)	222.8	53	99.9	$17,445	$21,836	$135,817	$175,098	
No (N = 2,715)	0	97.2	122.5	0	$40,046	$166,542	$206,589	

Note: Primary care cost estimate: $78.30 per visit; emergency room cost estimate: $412.00 per visit; other visit cost estimate: $1,359.53 per visit.

19.   Anil Bamezai, Glenn Melnick, and Amar Nawathe, "The Cost of an Emergency Department Visit and Its Relationship to Emergency Department Volume," *Annals of Emergency Medicine* 45, no. 5 (May 2005): 483–90.
20.   Hadley and Holahan, "The Cost of Care for the Uninsured."

Table 4.8 supports the conclusion that organizing care around primary care is a cost-effective strategy. All three VODI care strategies demonstrated cost savings. The greatest savings was for people without frequent ER use. The savings for enrollees who went to their assigned medical home was estimated at nearly $580 per enrollee. Preventing frequent emergency room use was also a cost-effective strategy, with an estimated annual savings of $1,052 per enrollee. Finally, the effort to transition enrollees from the emergency room to a medical home saved roughly $315 per enrollee. Because the groups in this analysis may overlap with one another, the savings are not cumulative. The percentage savings of these programs is substantial, ranging from 26% to 8%. Based on a total non–primary care cost estimate of $13,080,012 for 8,585 active enrollees, medical home use saved $2,223,602 annually. Savings from reduced emergency room use could exceed $500,000 (26% of $1.8 million in annual emergency room costs for the VODI population). Thus, organizing coverage and care for the uninsured can produce substantial cost savings.

Question 4: Which Enrollee Characteristics Were Associated with the Outcome Goals?

To better meet patient needs and design interventions to facilitate improved primary care utilization and reduce avoidable emergency room utilization, it is important to understand which factors influence care-seeking behavior. Hadley and Cunningham[21] found that age, gender, family structure, income, education, race/ethnicity, and attitude toward risk significantly influenced care-seeking behavior. In addition, having insurance and reducing out-of-pocket cost, along with having a regular source of care, increased the odds of a making physician visit. The VODI project addressed this question by asking whether demographics, economic status, and health status (i.e., having at least one qualifying chronic condition) were relevant to the VODI population. Did they influence the three primary outcomes of the organized care and delivery system? To address these questions, variables affecting health care, seeking, and utilization patterns were examined using negative binomial regression analysis. The exposure variables included gender, age, marital status, monthly household income, hours worked per week, number in household, and the presence of a chronic condition. Because the information for the chronic condition variable came from another form filled out at the time of enrollment (the Health Risk Appraisal form used in the disease management screening process, discussed in Chapter

---

21.   Hadley and Cunningham, "Availability of Safety Net Providers and Access to Care of Uninsured Persons."

5) and was not available for all active enrollees these models were restricted to a smaller number of clients. This resulted in smaller sample sizes of approximately 4,400 for the models with all types of enrollees and 3,000 for active emergency room enrollees. The regression models were created relative to three dependent variables: primary care visits, emergency room visits, and primary care visits for emergency room enrollees only. These are outlined in Table 4.9. Note the Incidence Rate Ratio (IRR) for the outcome variables listed in the table.

Primary care visits for all active enrollees was positively associated with monthly household income of $501–$1,000 and $1,001 or more (IRR = 1.56, 1.60), female gender (IRR = 1.43), chronic condition (IRR = 1.29), and age (IRR = 1.02) and was negatively associated with full-time employment, defined as 30 hours or more worked per week (IRR = 0.80). It was not significantly associated with marital status, number in household, or part-time employment (less than 30 hours worked per week).

Emergency room visits for all active enrollees was positively associated with part-time and full-time employment, as compared to no employment (IRR = 1.25, 1.38), and was negatively associated with age (IRR = 0.99), monthly household income of $1,001 or more (IRR = 0.79), and female gender (IRR = 0.70). It was not significantly associated with marital status, intermediate income ($501–$1,000 per month), number in household, or chronic condition.

The number of primary care visits for active emergency room enrollees was positively associated with higher and intermediate levels of income level (IRR = 1.78, 1.95), chronic condition (IRR = 1.37), female gender (IRR = 1.33), marital status (IRR = 1.17), and age (IRR = 1.02) and was negatively associated with full-time employment (IRR = 0.70). It was not significantly associated with working less than 30 hours per week or number in household.

Table 4.9. Negative Binominal Regression by Dependent Variable

Independent Variables	Dependent Variables								
	Primary Care Visits, All Active Enrollees (*N* = 4,439)			Emergency Room Visits, All Active Enrollees (*N* = 4,439)			Primary Care Visits, Active Emergency Room Enrollees (*N* = 3,020)		
	IRR*	CI IRR*	% CH	IRR*	CI IRR*	% CH	IRR*	CI IRR*	% CH
Gender									
Female	**1.43**	**1.30-1.56**	42.6	**0.70**	**0.62-0.79**	-30.2	**1.33**	**1.18-1.49**	32.8
Male	REF			REF			REF		
Age									
Continuous variable (in years)	**1.02**	**1.02-1.02**	2.0	0.99	0.98-1.00	-1.0	**1.02**	**1.01-1.02**	1.8
Marital status									
Not married	REF			REF			REF		
Married	1.10	0.99-1.22	9.8	0.91	0.78-1.05	-9.2	**1.17**	**1.02-1.34**	16.9
Total monthly household income									
$0-$500	REF			REF			REF		
$501-$1,000	**1.56**	**1.37-1.77**	55.6	0.88	0.73-1.04	-12.5	**1.78**	**1.50-2.12**	77.9
$1,001+	**1.60**	**1.39-1.84**	60.2	**0.79**	**0.65-0.95**	-21.3	**1.95**	**1.62-2.34**	95.2
Hours worked per week									
Unemployed	REF			REF			REF		
30 hours or less	0.91	0.80-1.05	-8.2	**1.25**	**1.04-1.51**	25.0	0.93	0.77-1.11	-7.4
30 hours or more	**0.80**	**0.72-0.90**	-19.5	**1.38**	**1.19-1.61**	38.4	**0.70**	**0.61-0.81**	-29.7
Number in household									
1 person	REF			REF			REF		
2 people	1.13	0.99-1.28	12.7	0.85	0.71-1.02	-14.8	1.14	0.97-1.35	14.3
3 or more people	1.06	0.94-1.20	6.0	0.94	0.80-1.10	-6.1	1.03	0.88-1.21	3.1
Chronic condition									
Yes	**1.29**	**1.17-1.42**	28.9	1.11	0.98-1.26	10.9	**1.37**	**1.21-1.56**	37.3
No	REF			REF			REF		

* Incidence rate ratio.

** 95% confidence internal for incidence rate ratio.

%CH=Percent Change

REF=referent

Conclusion

In summary, the VODI Intervention Model demonstrated increased access to the full continuum health care services. This resulted in increased primary care utilization and a reduction in emergency room use for enrollees who used the primary care medical home, thus giving them a regular source of care and reducing inpatient/specialty care. The patterns of care encouraged by the VODI Intervention Model are cost-effective. Savings of 17% were observed for medical home users compared to non–medical home users. Anecdotal evidence reported by patients and providers and patient satisfaction surveys suggest that more appropriate utilization of health services and improved health outcomes resulted from the implementation of the VODI Intervention Model.

Additional conclusions are:

- The type of enrollment location—emergency room or primary care site—was strongly related to subsequent utilization. This is consistent with the findings of Diehr[22] (1999), who has stated that "a strong predictor of future utilization is previous utilization." However, emergency room enrollees who went to their assigned primary care medical home on their first visit after enrollment—effectively transitioning to primary care—had more optimal patterns of use (decreased emergency room and specialty/inpatient care use) compared to those who did not transition to primary care.

- Certain demographic, socioeconomic, and health status factors were associated with health care utilization. Age, gender, income, and number of hours worked per week may all influence an individual's utilization of emergency room or primary care services. Those who are younger, male, and have low incomes show greater emergency room utilization and lower primary care utilization and may need to have interventions tailored around those factors.

- The finding that those who work more hours per week have a higher rate of emergency room use and a lower rate of primary care use suggests that a lack of convenient primary care office hours is a barrier to care. Increasing after-hours or nontraditional primary care office hours may be helpful.

---

22.   Diehr, D., Yanez, A., Ash, M., Hornbrook, and D. Y. Lin, "Methods for analyzing Health Care Utilization and Costs." Annual Review of Publilc Health 20. (May, 1999): 125-44

- Health status was examined by comparing those with at least one qualifying chronic condition to those without such conditions. As expected, those with at least one chronic condition had significantly higher primary care use rates but not lower emergency room use rates. Although those with chronic conditions may be increasing their use of primary care, they are still using the emergency room as they get their chronic condition under control. Given we tracked only a year of follow up post enrollment into VODI, we expect the complete transition to primary care to be longer for the chronically ill and over time, emergency room use should decrease.

- Because the uninsured are more likely to delay seeking care, it is critical to include structured access to specialty and other hospital-based diagnostic, ancillary, and surgical procedures. This is especially true for those with chronic conditions that may worsen without a regular source of care.

Lessons Learned

Lesson 1: Successful collaboration and coordination will lead to a more organized, uniform, and integrated coverage and care system.

- Care must be organized both vertically (within networks) and horizontally (among networks).

- All partners must agree to a set of similar benefits and implement a model of care that emphasizes the primary care/ medical home concept and access to a full continuum of care.

- Delivery system solutions need to fill health service gaps and link people to coverage and care.

- Primary care is the vital link in organizing care.

- Care is delivered locally, and therefore it must be organized locally.

- Specialty care referrals and payments are ongoing concerns for safety net primary care providers; this is a public policy gap that needs to be addressed at the national level.

Lesson 2: Organizing care delivery into "managed care" networks facilitates access to the full continuum of care. In the VODI networks, care providers agreed to provide "their share" of care for a specified number of uninsured patients.

- They were assured that patients would have access to other needed services.

- They could see others volunteering and participating in the care of the uninsured (the fellowship phenomenon).

- They could see their part in the full continuum of care.

Lesson 3: Intervening with the assignment and use of a medical home resulted in increased primary care use, cost-effective care, reduced emergency room use, and reduced inpatient/specialty care.

5

VODI Care and Disease Management Programs

Figure 5.1. VODI Intervention Model (VIM): 4Cs

- Organize Collaboration
  - The framework for building agreement and commitment.
    - SJHS/HFHS/DMC/OHS/DHD/WCHD/WSU/FQHC
- Organize Coordination
  - Working together in a common effort developing a common set of services and activities.
- Organize Coverage
  - Agreement to pay for a set of benefits to a defined population.
    - Registration
    - Enrollment
    - Medical Home Assignment
    - Tracking
    - Data Collection and Analysis
- Organize **Care**
  - The direct provision of services.
    - Medical Home Use
    - Basic Services: PC/Pharmacy/Lab/Dental
    - **Care Management**
    - **Disease Management**
    - Specialty Care/Ancillary and Diagnostic Services
    - Hospitalization

> •Care Management
> •Disease Management

↑**PC** ↓**ER** ↓**SC/Inpatient**

PC=Primary Care; ER=Emergency Room; SC=Specialty/Ancill/Diag Care

In Chapter 3, we discussed VODI's efforts to address the financing and insurance (coverage) component of health care reform. Chapter 4 discussed how VODI organized the delivery system (care) and succeeded at changing the care utilization patterns of VODI enrollees. In this chapter, we look at the third component of health care reform—facilitating behavioral and lifestyle change among patients and communities—and examine its relationship to care utilization patterns and cost-effective care for the uninsured. The definition of health advanced by VODI in chapter two was a holistic one that recognized health and well being as a combined function of favorable mental, physical, social, economic, environmental, behavioral, and community factors. Therefore individuals who live in poverty with associated joblessness resulting in vulnerable and fragile communities with disrupted social structures, have low educational attainment live in communities of high crime, with poor health indicators are not by our definition of health, in a state of well being. Given that many of VODI's enrollees might fit these demographics, we recognized that to improve health status and achieve VODI's goals, additional support services would be needed. Services to address these risk factors occurred through the development and implementation of the VODI care and disease management components of the VODI health care delivery model.

This chapter asks whether the addition of disease management services specifically targeted to the chronically ill and those with high-risk behaviors influenced patients' access to care and utilization patterns and produced cost savings. Therefore, this chapter compares rates of overall service utilization, emergency room utilization, primary care utilization, and transition from emergency to primary care, for a VODI disease management cohort to a non–disease management cohort. Although it was very difficult to enroll and sustain this population into a Disease Management Program, by managing this high-risk, chronically ill population, primary care use was enhanced by 100%.

The VODI Intervention Model included both care management and disease management services, as illustrated in Figure 5.1. Care management services were organized into a Care Management Program that was provided directly by the VODI partner networks. Disease management services were organized into a Disease Management Program that was provided by VODI's centralized disease management team. In this chapter, we explain and discuss both programs, focusing primarily on the disease management program. The analysis was structured so as to assess its impact (using a sample of VODI enrollees with specific chronic diseases or use patterns) on overall service utilization, emergency room utilization, primary care utilization, transition from emergency to primary care, and cost of care.

VODI and its partners received a Community Access Program (CAP) grant from the Health Resources and Services Administration to develop, implement, and evaluate the impact of a disease management program for high-risk VODI enrollees (see Figures 5.2 and 5.3). The disease management program was essentially a care management approach that focused on specific chronic diseases and use patterns and served as a focused expansion of the

VODI Care Management Program. The definition of "disease management" that VODI elected to use describes this practice "as a continuous, coordinated health care process that seeks to treat, manage and improve the health status of people with specific diseases or a carefully defined patient population over the entire course of a disease. The patient populations targeted are high-risk, high-cost patients with chronic conditions that depend on the development of a prospective, comprehensive and integrated treatment plan that maximizes patients function and quality of life through disease-specific management, education and supportive care."[1]

The VODI disease management program comprised services such as education about the patient's disease, education about diet and medication, help with appointments or health system navigation, referrals to community resources, help with prescriptions, and transportation and home visit assessments. The premise was that by investing in these disease management services, which were aimed at modifying the lifestyle and behavior patterns of patients with chronic diseases or high-risk behaviors, the VODI Intervention Model could further improve on the outcomes outlined in Chapter 4 and thus get patients to the right place, at the right time, for the right level of care. At its core, the VODI disease management program was about organizing the delivery system (organizing care). The disease management program targeted four diseases—hypertension, diabetes, asthma, and cancer—and the high-risk population of frequent emergency room users.

Figure 5.2. VODI Care & Disease Management Programs

VODI Partner Networks

Care Management
(Provided to all 18,838 VODI enrollees)

- Medical services
- Social Services
- Economic
- Continuity
- Health Education

VODI Central Administration

Disease Management (1,448 VODI Enrollees)

- Chronic Illnesses/High Risk:
  - Asthma
  - Cancer
  - Diabetes
  - Hypertension
  - Frequent ER users
- Services:
  - Disease specific education
  - Diet and medication education
  - Referrals to community resources
  - System navigation
  - Prescription assistance
  - Transportation assistance
  - Medical Home appointments

---

1.   This is the Disease Management Association of America's definition of disease management.

Figure 5.3. VODI Care & Disease Management Programs

VODI Partner Networks
VODI Care Management Program

VODI Care Management
(All of VODI Population)
18,838

Medical Services

Social Services

Economic Services

Continuity of Care

Health Education

VODI Central Administration
VODI Disease Management Program

Chronic Disease Study Population 1,448
•Asthma
•Cancer
•Diabetes
•Hypertension
•Frequent ER users
    Services
    •Disease specific Education
    •Disease specific Diet & medication education
    •Referrals to community resources
    •System navigation
    •Prescription assistance
    •Transportation assistance
    •Medical Home appointments

The VODI Care Management Program, a component of the VODI Intervention Model, comprised medical, social, economic, and educational services and the full continuum of care. These were delegated services provided by the VODI partners. Understand that all VODI enrollees received the Care Management Program. Only those enrollees with a chronic disease or high-risk behavior were eligible to receive the disease management program services. The disease management program services were standardized and provided by the VODI centralized disease management team. Although each VODI partner agreed to provide the full continuum of comprehensive quality care management services to each of the assigned 18,838 VODI enrollees, we did not normalize the Care Management Program across the partner networks. Instead, we relied on each VODI partner network's clinical quality care management standards and protocols. For this reason, we could not measure the impact of care management provided to VODI enrollees with as much precision and validity.

The VODI disease management program was developed with standardized services for a sample of eligible VODI enrollees with chronic diseases or high-risk behaviors (high emergency room users) so that we could more correctly measure its impact on primary care, emergency room, and inpatient/specialty care use for these populations. The premise was simple: Providing disease management services to high-risk, chronically

ill VODI enrollees would further improve on the targeted outcomes of the VODI Intervention Model.

The focus of the VODI disease management program was the early discovery of people with self-reported chronic diseases so that they could be empowered to use needed health care services and learn how to stay healthy through lifestyle choices. The behavioral and environmental changes induced by our disease management program were implemented in such a way as to have staying power, with the goal of obtaining a lasting effect and, ultimately, to achieve a positive shift in communities' health norms.

The Disease Management Team consisted of a manager, three nurses, three outreach workers, and one social worker. This team provided an intervention aimed at improving the health status of enrollees and reducing the amount of long-term disability resulting from their conditions. Similarly, VODI enrollees who reported a high number of emergency room visits or missed health care appointments in the six months prior to enrollment into VODI were also included in the VODI disease management program. The Disease Management Team would help ensure that these enrollees were established with a primary care medical home and received appropriate health care. As a result, these enrollees could also access a continuum of health care, and the direct costs associated with suboptimal emergency room could be reduced.

Background: Why Is Chronic Disease Management Important?

The United States is experiencing an epidemic unlike any in its history. With an annual financial burden of more than $350 billion, chronic diseases are now responsible for three out of every four deaths in the United States, in contrast to infectious diseases, which drove morbidity and mortality in the beginning of the 20th century.[2,3] However, "the impact of chronic diseases extends beyond mortality. It also has a significant impact on morbidity, with over 100 million Americans, one-third of the U.S. population, experiencing some level of disability or severe limitation in their daily activities due to chronic disease. It is projected that by 2010, 120 million Americans will be affected by morbidity and up to 134 million by the year 2020. By then it is estimated, the U.S. cost associated with the chronic disease epidemic will approach $1 trillion dollars annually."[4]

---

2.   Michael Siegel and Lynne Doner, *Marketing Public Health: Strategies to Promote Social Change* (Gaithersburg, MD: Aspen, 1998).

3.   Brian D. Smedley, Adrienne Y. Stith, and Alan R. Nelson, eds., *Unequal Treatment: Confronting Racial and Ethnic Disparities in Health Care* (Washington, DC: National Academy Press, 2002).

4.   Siegel and Doner, *Marketing Public Health*.

Unhealthy lifestyles and behaviors are driving this epidemic, along with deteriorating social and economic conditions, worsening health disparities, and a crisis in access to quality health care in many segments of U.S. society.[5, 6] The medical model alone cannot solve the chronic disease epidemic, and as a country, we must focus on more than just the provision of medical care in order to truly address the public's health. If we are to stop the 21st-century epidemic of chronic disease, we must, first and foremost, dedicate our efforts and resources to modifying individual lifestyle and behavior choices, improving the socioeconomic and environmental conditions of communities, and providing all Americans with basic access to quality health care.

In Michigan, as in the nation, chronic diseases are among the most common and costly diseases, but they are also the most preventable. In Michigan, two out of every three deaths are caused by one of five chronic diseases: heart disease, cancer, stroke, chronic lower respiratory disease, and diabetes. However, the real causes of these chronic diseases are tobacco use, physical inactivity, overweight, and obesity. Tobacco use is the number one cause of preventable deaths in Michigan: About one-quarter of adults and one-quarter of high school students in Michigan smoke. This amounts to 1.9 million smokers out of a total population of 9.8 million, including 174,000 children. The second and third leading causes of preventable death in Michigan are obesity and physical inactivity: Approximately 61% of Michigan adults are overweight or obese. The total costs associated with tobacco use, obesity, and physical inactivity—including medical care costs, lost productivity and workers compensation claims—are conservatively estimated at more than $20 billion dollars per year, with 70% of all deaths in Michigan and 70% of the total health care cost in the state related to chronic diseases.[7]

A Michigan Economic Development Corporation study[8] showed that, compared to similar states, Michigan has the highest rate of death from heart disease; ranks second in obesity and diabetes rates; and ranks sixth in smoking rates. This study concluded that the "unhealthy lifestyles of Michigan residents make them vulnerable to heart disease and diabetes, major factors that drive up the cost of health care in Michigan."[9] Investing

5.   Smedley, Stith, and Nelson, *Unequal Treatment*.

6.   Ibid.

7.   M. L. Cook and A. P. Rafferty, *Health Risk Behaviors in the State of Michigan: 2004 Behavioral Risk Factor Survey, 18th Annual Report* (Lansing MI: Michigan Department of Community Health, Bureau of Epidemiology Services Division, 2005).

8.   James Bologna, Paul Hughes-Cromwick, and Charles Roehrig, *Healthcare Costs and Premiums: Michigan Compared with Selected Benchmarked States* (Lansing: Michigan Economic Development Corporation, 2004).

9.   Ibid.

in resources to modify lifestyle and behavioral choices—and therefore chronic disease prevention—can save lives and dollars and improve the health of the people of the state while improving the health of Michigan's budget. It is a win–win proposal for the public health and the fiscal health of a community.

The reduction of unhealthy lifestyles has become an increasingly important dimension of health care as chronic and degenerative diseases have displaced acute, communicable diseases as the leading causes of morbidity and mortality in the United States. Because of the high direct and indirect costs associated with chronic diseases, the VODI project developed programs to intervene to improve the access, quality, and costs of health care for VODI enrollees with chronic diseases.

The need to avert costs and improve health outcomes of VODI enrollees prompted the partners to acquire grant resources from the American Legacy Foundation for a VODI smoking cessation program. As discussed earlier, tobacco use is the number one cause of preventable deaths in Michigan and the United States and the number one contributor to chronic disease in Michigan. Therefore, the smoking cessation program was believed to be critical to chronic disease modification and it provided services to VODI enrollees who were current smokers.

Who Was Enrolled?

Of 18,838 VODI enrollees, 2,714 enrollees were identified as qualifying for the disease management program during the 2003 and 2004 enrollment years. To better give an idea of the full scope of disease management activities that were conducted, the analyses that quantify services provided to these enrollees are based on the 2003–2004 cohort. However, the comparison of utilization rates is limited to the 15,421 enrollees who were enrolled before January 1, 2004, as only those enrollees had a full 12 months of service data available for inclusion in the analysis. As a result, 1,448 of the 15,421 were included in an impact analysis for the VODI disease management program, as this subpopulation met the disease management program eligibility criteria and had 12 months of service data after their 2003 VODI enrollment.

Figure 5.4. Analytic Framework for Studying VODI Intervention Model (VIM) Impact

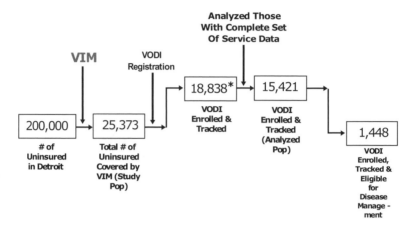

*18,838 enrollees are people who were enrolled & tracked but for whom we did not have a full 12 months of service data to include them in the impact analysis. We analyzed **15,241** of the 18,838 VODI enrolled & tracked who had a complete 12 months of service data allowing full VIM impact analysis.

The characteristics of VODI enrollees by participant status in the disease management program are reported in Table 5.1. These characteristics were collected in order to establish whether participants and non-participants were similar enough to make valid comparisons. The results show that the disease management cohort had more females, more enrollees with a greater number of qualifying chronic diseases, fewer enrollees who were frequent emergency room users, and fewer asthmatics than in the non–disease management cohort. Chi-square and Fisher exact tests were used to determine the statistically significant differences.

Table 5.1. Characteristics of VODI Disease Management Eligible Enrollees, 2003-2004 Cohort

	Disease Management Participants		Non-Disease Management Participants	
	Number	Percent	Number	Percent
Enrollment location				
Emergency room	74	56.9	1,656	63.3
Other	7	5.4	77	3.0
Primary care setting	49	37.7	882	33.7
Total	130	100.0	2,615	100.0
Gender				
Female	84	65.1	1,482	56.8
Male	45	34.9	1,126	43.2
Total	129	100.0	2,608	100.0

Table 5.1. Characteristics of VODI Disease Management Eligible Enrollees, 2003-2004 Cohort (Continued)

	Disease Management Participants		Non-Disease Management Participants	
	Number	Percent	Number	Percent
Age*				
18-29	17	13.1	492	18.8
30-44	41	31.5	954	36.5
45-64	72	55.4	1,169	44.7
Total	130	100.0	2,615	100.0
Marital status				
Divorced	13	10.1	319	12.2
Married	24	18.6	447	17.1
Separated	7	5.4	145	5.6
Single	81	62.8	1,600	61.4
Widowed	4	3.1	97	3.7
Total	129	100.0	2,608	100.0
Ethnicity				
Arab American	0	0	8	0.3
Asian American	0	0	10	0.4
African American	120	95.2	2,223	90.3
Hispanic	2	1.6	117	4.8
Multiracial	0	0	3	0.1
Native American/Indian	0	0	8	0.3
Other	0	0	5	0.2
White	4	3.2	89	3.6
Total	126	100.0	2,463	100.0
Total monthly household income				
$0-$500	21	16.3	587	22.5
$501-$1,000	59	45.7	1,069	41.0
$1,001 or more	49	38.0	951	36.5
Total	129	100.0	2,607	100.0
Hours worked per week				
Unemployed	59	45.4	1,254	48.0
30 hours or less	22	16.9	383	14.6
30 hours or more	49	37.7	977	37.4
Total	130	100.0	2,614	100.0
Number in household				
1 person	29	22.3	656	25.1
2 people	34	26.2	686	26.2
3 or more people	67	51.5	1,272	48.7
Total	130	100.0	2,614	100.0
Number of chronic conditions**				
No conditions with frequent emergency room use	3	2.3	223	8.6
1 condition with or without frequent emergency room use	88	67.7	1,823	70.0

Table 5.1. Characteristics of VODI Disease Management Eligible Enrollees, 2003-2004 Cohort (Continued)

	Disease Management Participants		Non-Disease Management Participants	
	Number	Percent	Number	Percent
Number of chronic conditions**				
2 or more conditions with or without frequent emergency room use	39	30.0	558	21.4
Total	130	100.0	2,604	100.0
Qualifying condition***				
Asthma	17	13.1	541	20.8
Cancer	1	0.8	24	0.9
Diabetes	13	10.0	221	8.5
Frequent Emergency Room Use Only	3	2.3	223	8.6
Hypertension	57	43.8	1,037	39.8
More than one qualifying chronic condition	39	30.0	558	21.4
Total	130	100.0	2,604	100.0

* Chi-square = 6.16; df = 2; p-value = 0.046

** Chi-square = 10.1; df = 2; p-value = 0.006

*** Chi-square and Fisher's exact tests were used on individual two-by-two tables that were constructed to compare the proportions for each level (row) of this variable. The Chi-square test comparing the proportions with and without a single qualifying chronic condition of asthma (Chi-square = 4.43; df = 1; p-value = 0.0353) and with and without multiple qualifying chronic conditions (Chi-square = 5.46; df = 1; p-value = 0.020) were statistically significant. The Fisher exact test for enrollees with or without frequent emergency room use (p-value = 0.008) was also statistically significant. Other Chi-square and Fisher's exact tests were not statistically significant.

The fact that only 4.8% ($N = 130$) of the 2,714 enrollees who completed a Health Risk Appraisal and qualified for the disease management program agreed to participate in the program underscores the difficulty of trying to reach this population (see Table 5.2). The small sample size for the disease management participants who only had frequent emergency room use as their qualifying condition is consistent with the finding that moving frequent emergency room users out of the emergency room is extremely difficult (see Chapter 4). These findings show that the effort required to engage VODI enrollees in a disease management program was considerable.

Table 5.2. Percent of Enrollees in the VODI Disease
Management Program, 2003-2004 Cohort

VODI Enrollees	Health Risk Appraisals Completed	Health Risk Appraisals Meeting Eligibility Criteria	Enrollees with Case Opened	
			N	Percent of Those Eligible
7,926	6,688	2,714	130	4.8

What Was Done?

The VODI disease management program offered a wide variety and greater intensity of services to its participants. This process involved the identification of eligible participants; the identification of participants' needs; and tailored interventions to help VODI enrollees meet those needs. A holistic approach was used to determine health care need, as social factors may also affect the health status and health care utilization patterns of patients. The approach relied primarily on education and referral of enrollees to health care and social services.

The education component involved the provision of information on many different health issues, such as information on chronic conditions self-reported on the Health Risk Appraisal and on medications that the enrollees were using to treat their condition(s). It also involved demonstrating the use of medical equipment, such as blood pressure cuffs, peak flow meters, and glucometers, and educating enrollees about optimal ways to navigate the health system, pharmacy procedures and resources, and eligibility for other health insurance programs. Healthier lifestyle choices, including exercise, nutrition, and reducing or quitting tobacco use, were also encouraged as part of the education process.

A number of other services were also offered through VODI Disease Management Program. This included advocacy within the health system, navigation through the continuum of care, assistance with mental health and community referrals, distribution of free medical equipment (blood pressure cuffs, peak flow meters, and glucometers), and provision of short-term intervention and problem solving. Additional services were also provided by connecting enrollees with community resources and making referrals to a number of other providers, including nutritionists, oral health providers and dentists, low-cost vision care, prescription assistance, and the Department of Health and Human Resources (formerly the Family Independence Agency) for Medicaid or Supplemental Security Income.

In order to identify participants, enrollees were screened for eligibility criteria using a one-page Health Risk Appraisal form at the time of enrollment in the VODI program. The appraisal asked questions on five main topics (see Figure 5.5). This allowed the identification of enrollees with qualifying chronic conditions or frequent emergency room use, as well as those who smoked, so that they could be contacted for follow-up.

Figure 5.5. Health Risk Appraisal

Enroll Site: _____   VODI # _____

Voices of Detroit Initiative (VODI)
Health Risk Appraisal for Care Management – Selected Chronic Conditions

Name: _____   Date of birth: _____Today's Date: _____
Address: _____   Sex (Circle): M   F   Doctor: _____
_____ Zip code: _____   Social Security #: _____
Telephone #: _____   Center assigned: _____

A. Health Status

1. Have you been told by a doctor that you have **High Blood Pressure**?	**YES** (1)	**NO** (0)
2. Have you been told by a doctor that you have **High Blood Sugar (Diabetes)**?	**YES** (1)	**NO** (0)
3. Have you been told by a doctor that you have **Asthma**?	**YES** (1)	**NO** (0)
4. Have you been told by a doctor that you have **Cancer**?	**YES** (1)	**NO** (0)
If you answered YES, what type of cancer? _____		

B. If you answered YES to one or more of the above:

5. Are you interested in learning more about how you can manage your disease?	**YES** (1)	**NO** (0)
6. Do you have a hard time getting the health care services that you need?	**YES** (1)	**NO** (0)
7. Have you ever delayed taking your prescription medication, or taken less than ordered, due to cost?	**YES** (1)	**NO** (0)
8. Do you need assistance obtaining medical supplies for one or more of the above conditions?	**YES** (1)	**NO** (0)
9. Do you need help with other non-medical issues that make it difficult for you to stay in control of your	**YES** (1)	**NO** (0)

health?   **Please specify:** _____

10. Do you currently smoke **cigarettes**?	**Not at all** (0)	**Some days** (1)	**Every day** (3)

11. Do you currently drink **alcohol**?	**Not at all** (0)	**Some days** (1)	**Every day** (2)

12. Can you count on anyone to provide you with **emotional support**, such as talking over problems or helping you make a difficult decision?	**YES** (0)	**NO** (1)	**Do not need Help** (0)

C. Utilization:
13. In the **last 6 months**:

a. Have you scheduled a doctor's appointment?	**No** (1)	**Yes, once.** (0)	**Yes, 2 or more times.** (1)
b. Have you missed a scheduled doctor's appointment?	**No** (0)	**Yes, once.** (1)	**Yes, 2 or more times.** (2)
c. Have you been to the emergency room?	**No** (0)	**Yes, once.** (1)	**Yes, 2 or more times.** (2)
d. Have you been hospitalized?	**No** (0)	**Yes, once.** (1)	**Yes, 2 or more times.** (2)

14. **Screening:** Have you had any of these exams/test within the last **12** months?

Cholesterol	**YES** (Date:) **NO**	**For Men Only:** Blood test for prostate	**YES** (Date:)	**NO**	
Dental exam	**YES** (Date:) **NO**	Cancer rectal exam	**YES** (Date:)	**NO**	
Colon test for blood	**YES** (Date:) **NO**	**For Women Only:** Breast Mammogram Pelvic/pap smear	**YES** (Date:) **YES** (Date:)	**NO** **NO**	

"I agree to have a care manager contact me for any future health care that I may need."

Signature: _____   Alternative phone number: _____

Personnel Only:
A Total: _____ (1)
B Total: _____ (5)
C Total: _____ (3)

HRA_Form
MsWord_5/22/01, modified 11/15/02

VODI enrollees who agreed to participate in the Disease Management Program were assessed using two screening tools that evaluated their medical history and social factors affecting their health care. A Nurse's Assessment collected comprehensive information about the client's medical history, while an Outreach Worker's Assessment collected information on the social needs of the enrollee. These two tools were used in conjunction with a Master Treatment Plan that was developed as a basic protocol for delivering services to enrollees.

Using information gleaned from the assessments, a nurse developed and tailored a Master Treatment Plan for each client in collaboration with VODI outreach personnel and the enrollee. This protocol was used to monitor the delivery of disease management services to the enrollee. Table 5.3 reports the disease management services that were identified as needed by individual enrollees and those provided to enrollees as part of the Disease Management Program in 2003–2004. Table 5.3 was constructed through the use of a database that tracked goals, tasks, and referrals made for each client. The information collected on short-term goals (tasks) and referrals was grouped into eight main items based on the short-term goals listed in the Master Treatment Plan.

Table 5.3. Top Disease Management Services Needed by and Provided to Enrollees, 2003-2004

Service	Need Identified		Services Provided	
	N	*Percent*	*N*	*Percent*
1. Education on disease (diabetes, hypertension, asthma, cancer)*	108	85.0	91	71.7
2. Education on diet or medication	116	89.2	98	75.4
3. Help with appointments or health system navigation	81	62.3	44	33.8
4. Referral to community resources (mental health** or basic needs)	76	58.5	64	49.2
5. Smoking cessation program	46	35.4	36	27.7
6. Help with prescription access	16	12.3	12	9.2
7. Transportation	7	5.4	5	3.8
8. Home visit assessment	0	0.0	0	0.0

* The denominator for calculating the percentages for this category was only 127 instead of the total 130 disease management enrollees, as three enrollees showed frequent emergency room use (not a chronic condition) as their only qualifying condition.
** For part of the period included in this evaluation, community referrals were also made internally to the VODI-CAP social worker.

**Table 5.4. All Disease Management Services Needed by
and Provided to Enrollees, 2003-2004**

Referral	N	Share of Enrollees with Open Cases
Assigned clinic for primary care physician follow-up	130	100.0
Nutrition/dietician	62	47.7
Dentist/oral health	56	43.1
Low-cost vision services	48	36.9
Assistance for food, clothing, or other basic needs	38	29.2
Smoking cessation	29	22.3
Medicaid, Supplemental Security Income, etc.	28	21.5
Prescription assistance	16	12.3
Employment/career	11	8.5
Free Quit Smoking Coaching Hotline	9	6.9
Transportation	7	5.4
Health care	7	5.4
Medical supplies	5	3.8
Assigned clinic for visit with primary care physician regarding Nicotine Replacement Therapy (NRT) /other smoking cessation therapy	5	3.8
Social services	5	3.8
Mental health or social services	4	3.1
Health education class	4	3.1
Breast and Cervical Cancer Control Program	3	2.3
Housing assistance	3	2.3
Cancer prevention/detection	2	1.5
Weight Watchers	2	1.5
Telephone services	1	0.8
Parenting classes	1	0.8
Substance abuse	1	0.8

* All Disease Management referrals examined here were from the period 2003:Q1–2004:Q4.

Referrals to other resources or health care providers were an integral part of the Disease Management Program; the most common referrals are presented in Table 5.4. In this case, the most common referrals were made to direct enrollees to their assigned primary care medical home for care, as this was typically recommended for all enrollees. The second most common referral was made for nutrition or diet counseling. Smaller percentages of enrollees received referrals involving dentist/oral health, assistance for basic needs, low-cost vision services, and other services. Referrals for education about the enrollee's disease were addressed by the VODI Disease Management Program staff.

In addition to the initial sessions for enrollee education and referrals, follow-up visits to note enrollees' progress was another important component to the services provided by the VODI team. By following up with enrollees, the Disease Management Team tracked the completion of tasks assigned or referrals given to the enrollees. In addition, it helped track the number of enrollees who reached their long-term goals. By monitoring and following up on medical appointments and medications, the Disease Management Team helped ensure that enrollees were receiving needed health care.

What Was the Impact?

As discussed in Chapter 4, we showed that we could change care utilization patterns and provide more cost-effective care to the uninsured by developing a coverage/benefit model and better organizing the delivery system. This chapter has asked whether adding eight disease management services specifically targeted at the chronically ill and those with high-risk behaviors could yield additional access to care and cost benefits, as well as further change utilization patterns for this population. All VODI enrollees received the VODI Intervention Model. Only those with chronic illnesses and those with high-risk behaviors received the additional VODI disease management services. Thus, this chapter compares the rates of overall service utilization, emergency room utilization, primary care utilization, transition from emergency to primary care, and the cost of care for a VODI disease management cohort compared to a eligible but non–disease management cohort.

To obtain this information, two methodologies were used. One methodology used a chart review that was carried out on 75 VODI Disease Management Program cases opened between January 1, 2003, and September 30, 2003. This chart review provided estimates for the number of contacts and referrals made per client, as well as the average length of time in the VODI Disease Management Program. This earlier analysis conducted to quantify the services typically received by disease management enrollees allowed for the determination of some basic service measures, including the average number of contacts per participant (3 contacts) and the average length of time in the program (3.5 months).[10] It also showed that a wide range of issues were managed by the VODI team for enrollees. In fact, some enrollees received up to nine referrals related to health care or basic needs, though the average number of referrals per enrollee was 2.5.

Figure 5.6.: Comparison of PC/ER/SS/Hosp Use based *Disease Mgmt Use* post VODI Intervention

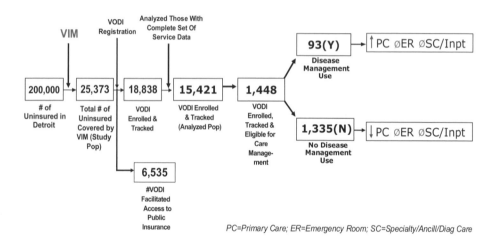

PC=Primary Care; ER=Emergency Room; SC=Specialty/Ancill/Diag Care

A number of additional analyses were also carried out to evaluate the effectiveness of the Disease Management Program. Figure 5.6 summarizes the algorithm used to compare primary care, emergency room, and inpatient/specialty care use for Disease Management Program participants use after the VODI intervention. This restriction limited the analysis to VODI enrollees who had at least one qualifying chronic disease or high-risk behavior, who were enrolled in 2003 with at least 12 months of service data, and who were eligible to receive disease management services. This subpopulation was further divided into cohorts for VODI Disease Management Program participants ($n = 93$) and non-participants ($n = 1,335$), as shown in Figure 5.6. This methodology constitutes a retrospective cohort analysis employing a non-participant cohort enrolled during the same time period (2003:Q1–2003:Q4) and having the same inclusion criteria used for

---

10. Variables with more than two levels were collapsed into two-by-two tables if at least one cell had fewer than five subjects. Chi-square tests were then carried out on resulting two-by-two tables. Fisher exact tests were carried out on two-by-two tables if at least one cell had fewer than five subjects.

the disease management participants to ensure more comparability between the groups. The inclusion criteria included a history of high blood pressure, diabetes mellitus, asthma, cancer or high emergency room utilization, as identified by the Health Risk Appraisal. Because the Health Risk Appraisal was completed at the time of enrollment, each enrollee also received a VODI identification number. This process allowed each enrollee to be tied to the VODI enrollment and service databases so that analyses using the latter two databases could also be conducted.

The source population ($N = 15,421$) included some enrollees who did not utilize any of the principal VODI services (primary, emergency, inpatient, and specialty care), as well as enrollees who did utilize at least one of these services. Rates were determined using this population so as to correct for the artificial inflation that may be seen when populations are restricted to those who have utilized services; in this way, a comparison to national norms may be made. A second source population ($N = 8,585$) that had only enrollees who utilized at least one of the principal VODI services after enrollment was also studied, although very similar results were obtained. (Refer to Appendix B for details of the analysis of this second study population).

The first study population of participants and non-participants was examined with a few different analyses. One compared the utilization rates for overall services, emergency room services, and primary care services between the cohorts. Similarly, both groups were examined for the percentage of emergency room enrollees who made a documented primary care visit at their assigned medical home following enrollment in the VODI program. Finally, the characteristics of the two cohorts were compared on 2003 enrollment statistics to further ensure the comparability of the two groups.

The analysis of characteristics of the two cohorts (not shown) repeated the same statistical tests to check for significant differences between the two groups, except that they were carried out on the 2003 enrollees only. These additional tests showed the same significant differences, except that the 2003 non-participants showed a significantly lower percentage of patients enrolled at primary care sites compared to the disease management participants (X2 = 6.89, df =2, p-value = 0.032).

Although the results show statistical significance, comparisons may still be made if the results are interpreted conservatively. For example, although a greater percentage of disease management participants had more than one qualifying chronic condition compared to non-participants, this difference may be expected to increase emergency room and inpatient/specialty care utilization, thereby underestimating the impact of the Disease Management Program. Furthermore, the category of disease management participants who had frequent emergency room use as their only eligibility criteria showed a very small sample size and, as a result, may not provide the most reliable estimate for comparison of this measure. Thus, the differences reported for the cohorts, regardless of whether the enrollment period was 2003 or 2003–2004, were not great enough to prevent a valid comparison of the two groups.

Table 5.5. Utilization Rates among Disease Management Participants Enrolled in 2003

	Utilization Rate (per 100 Members)							
	Cohort	Primary Care		Emergency Room		Specialty/ Inpatient Care		Overall	
No disease management received	1,355	99.9	1.0	49.3	0.5	93.6	0.9	242.9	2.4
Disease management received	93	198.9	2.0	52.7	0.5	91.4	0.9	343.0	3.4

Note: Both cohorts compared enrollees who were identified as having one or more of the four chronic conditions or a history of high emergency room utilization. Overall utilization includes primary care, emergency room, and inpatient/specialty care visits. Rates are based on service visits within one year of the enrollee's registration date, excluding visits on the actual date of enrollment.

Comparisons of the utilization rates of the two cohorts during the first year of participation in VODI by type of service received are presented in Table 5.5. The types of services examined include emergency care, primary care, and inpatient/specialty, as well as the overall rate. A standard methodology was used to determine these rates, such that the rate per member is simply the quotient obtained by taking the total number of service visits made during the first year of participation for each of the three categories and dividing each of the three totals by the number of members in the cohort. The rate per 100 is that quotient multiplied by 100 to get a utilization rate per 100 members. Both the rate per member and the rate per 100 members are presented here for ease of comparison with other results presented in the literature or available online from the Centers for Disease Control.

The methodology used here to look at utilization rates is consistent with that employed in earlier chapters of the book. This methodology only includes utilization data for the first 12 months post enrollment. (This methodology is discussed in more detail in Chapter 3).

Table 5.5 further shows that disease management enrollees had some notable differences in their utilization rates compared to eligible VODI participants who did not receive disease management. The overall utilization rate for the disease management participants was approximately 30% higher than those who did not participate in disease management. A review of the type of service visits, indicates that this increase may be attributable to a 100% increase in primary care rates for disease management participants compared to those who did not participate in disease management. There was no significant difference in the rates of emergency care and inpatient/specialty care, between the two cohorts compared.

Table 5.6 looks at the difference between VODI Disease Management Program participants and non-participants for the outcome related to transitioning enrollees from emergency care to an assigned primary care medical home. This refers to enrollees who initially registered through the emergency room and who used their assigned primary care medical home after their VODI registration date.

Table 5.6. Disease Management Participants Transitioned to Primary Care Medical Home

	Enrollees with Visit Following Enrollment	Emergency Room to Primary Care	
		Number	Percent
No disease management services received	545	261	47.9
Disease management services received	39	26	66.7

Note: Both cohorts compared enrollees who were identified as having one or more of the four conditions or a history of high emergency room utilization. Enrollees were enrolled between 2003: Q1 and 2003:Q4. The analysis used utilization data within 12 months of the date of enrollment, excluding visits on the actual date of enrollment. The non–disease management control group had 917 patients enrolled through the emergency room during this time period. The disease management group had 51 patients enrolled through the emergency room during this time period.

Conclusions

All VODI enrollees, regardless of whether they participated in the Disease Management Program, were a part of the VODI Intervention Model, which included coordination and organization of coverage and care with access to a defined set of core services (see Chapter 2). Consequently, the two different interventions of VODI (the VODI Intervention Model and the Disease Management program) supportively reinforced one another, and therefore a valid question may be if the two interventions have an additive effect.

Although it was difficult to enroll this population into the VODI Disease Management Program, we were able to show that for those who were enrolled, disease management further improved the impact of the VODI

Intervention Model by enhancing primary care use by an additional 100%. Emergency room and inpatient/specialty care use remained unchanged for the high-risk populations that were served by the disease management team. This is probably attributable to the fact that the VODI Disease Management Program primarily emphasized disease education, enhanced use of outpatient services, and enhanced facilitation of medical home use. The VODI Intervention Model had already made significant inroads in the reduction of emergency room and inpatient/specialty care utilization. Although the additional enhancement of primary care medical home use does not appear to have further lowered emergency room and inpatient/specialty care utilization rates during the one-year follow-up period, we believe this may not be enough time to see an impact; considered longitudinally, we would likely see decreases in emergency room and inpatient/specialty care use.

The VODI Disease Management Program increased primary care utilization rates and helped transition enrollees from emergency care to an assigned primary care medical home (Tables 5.5 and 5.6). Although the disease management cohort was shown to have more participants who were enrolled at a primary care site—itself a powerful predictor of primary care use—the finding that even emergency room enrollees participating in disease management had a higher rate of primary care use suggests that another process is likely involved.

Given the positive effect of the Disease Management Program on primary care utilization patterns of participants, several limitations should be mentioned. First, there is the possibility of selection bias, as those who chose to participate in the Disease Management Program may have been more compliant or engaged with the health care system before they enrolled in that specialized part of the VODI program. Second, the analysis of utilization rates did not take into account any possible confounding or interaction effects of third variables. Important third variables include the gender, age, and health status, as these may affect or influence a patient's compliance or degree of engagement with the health care system. Further analyses that control for these variables should be conducted when data from larger sample sizes is available.

Follow-Up Intervention

In light of the results of reported in Tables 5.5 and 5.6, a program was developed that was devoted exclusively to transitioning enrollees from the emergency room to an assigned primary care home. It was developed during the last half of 2004 and implemented in January 2005, outside the study time frame. This program, called the 24-Hour to 48-Hour Turnaround

Program, attempted to reach enrollees within 24–48 hours of their release from the emergency room, provided that they were not hospitalized. Efforts were then made to set up appointments for follow-up care with a primary care physician. The supposition was that more optimal utilization patterns may be promoted by directly establishing the enrollees with a primary care medical home and educating them about the proper navigation of the health care system. Results from this new approach were not available at the time of the writing of this book.

Lessons Learned

Lesson 1: It is difficult to engage low income patients with chronic conditions or frequent emergency room users in disease management programs; however, for those we did engage, primary care use was increased by 100%.

Lesson 2: Care management, which was provided to all VODI enrollees, and disease management, which was provided as an additional intervention to VODI enrollees with a chronic illness or high-risk behavior, had an additive impact.

Lesson 3: Specifically managing high-risk and chronically ill patients with a Disease Management Program is an essential part of organizing the health care delivery system, and it is a critical component in providing effective care to an uninsured population.

Lesson 4: Strengthening linkages with community support systems, agencies and services improves primary care use.

6

Lessons Learned and Policy Recommendations

Any journey, such as the path to health care reform, must be guided by a compass that provides accurate direction. The elements of the Voices of Detroit Initiative (VODI) model—collaboration, coordination, coverage, and care—provide such a compass. This book has described some of the obstacles that lay across our path in implementing VODI and how we successfully worked together as a community to overcome them. It has also measured VODI's impact on access to care and health care utilization patterns of those without health insurance. This chapter outlines the lessons learned and suggests policy recommendations for reform.

Lessons Learned
Collaboration and Coordination

Lesson 1: Getting the right people in the right structure is vital to achieving a workable consensus. The phrase "workable consensus" means that in order to be effective, a policy solution must both solve the problem and represent a consensus of stakeholders.

- The process of implementing this lesson requires surveying the community for organizations that are critical to success, recruiting leaders from organizations that can commit resources to the effort, and building consensus through a structure that engages operational experts who can devise feasible work plans. One advantage of this approach is that it provides a forum for leaders to settle issues that impede progress, thereby reducing the time spent on issues that are not related to action steps. Building a workable consensus requires discussion and approval of feasible action steps. The collaborative structure and processes need to be more formal and official early in the initiative and can become less formal over time as trust builds.

- Developing a path to change requires inclusiveness and critical stakeholder investment, involvement, and collaboration. Organizing a formal structure and applying meeting tools to create a safe environment for open and authentic dialogue is critical for flushing out areas of agreement and resolving areas of disagreement to achieve desired outcomes. The time needed for agreement is generally underestimated. Levels of agreement ebb and flow over time. Patience is important. The collaborative meeting table needs to be round; the collaborative must address underlying interests and work toward mutual benefits and gains in order to move the process forward.

Lesson 2: If collaboration is going to lead to action, agreement is more important than the size of the step.

- Collaboration is an iterative and cumulative process. Partners must collaboratively agree on what success will look like. As members resolve issues and agree on common action steps, trust is built and the number of controversies declines. Over time, stronger relationships are built through repeated acts of trust.

- Collaboration and coordination are not simply leadership functions. Collaboration and coordination must occur within and across partner organizations.

- Leadership and a funding catalyst are very important to launching and sustaining an effort. As agreements cumulate, collaboration and coordination are organized and the structure becomes more permanent. A permanent structure made VODI more resilient to the constantly changing local and national health care environment.

Lesson 3: Relationships, responsibility, accountability, and transparency—created through collaboration and coordination—are the link between agreement and execution. The key to successfully reaching goals is to balance results (completion of the task), process (how work gets done), and relationships (how people's involvement and contributions are validated and valued).

Lesson 4: Reporting mechanisms, such as benchmark-driven scorecards, improve accountability and transparency within the collaborative and move the project forward. The scorecard is a useful device for tracking progress and deliberating future actions. The discussion of scorecard results at the policy-making level helps maintain consensus and focuses action on goals.

Coverage

Lesson 1: A significant benefit from screening the uninsured is the identification of people who are eligible for insurance. Coordinating public and private insurance information is essential to reduce the number of uninsured.

Lesson 2: Collaboration and coordination make it possible to build an information system that can identify, track, and monitor care for the uninsured. Such an information system is a foundation for successful and supportive community interventions to manage the care of those without health insurance.

Lesson 3: Organizing coverage and care must be done in concert. The organization of coverage and care must be coordinated. Simply providing a coverage mechanism without organizing the delivery system at the local level will not result in the uninsured getting the care they need or that unnecessary costs are controlled.

- Insurance coverage is critical but not sufficient for access and appropriate service utilization. The mere existence of coverage does not necessarily ensure access to care or guarantee that care will be rendered appropriately. Furthermore, the existence of safety net services does not necessarily mean that services will be used or used appropriately.

- National and state reforms are implemented at the community level. Therefore, community-driven solutions are imperative if reforms are to be successful.

Care

Lesson 1: Successful collaboration and coordination will lead to a more organized, standardized and integrated coverage and care system.

- Care must be organized both vertically (within networks) and horizontally (among networks).

- All partners must agree to a set of similar benefits and implement a model of care that emphasizes the primary care medical home concept and access to a full continuum of care.

- Delivery system solutions need to both fill health service gaps and link people to coverage and care.

- Primary care is the vital link in organizing care.

- Care is delivered locally, and therefore it must be organized locally.

- Specialty care referrals and payments are ongoing concerns for safety net primary care providers; this is a public policy gap that needs to be addressed at the national level.

Lesson 2: Organizing care delivery into virtual "managed care" networks facilitates access to the full continuum of care. In the VODI networks, care providers agreed to provide "their share" of care for a specified number of uninsured patients.

- They were assured that patients would have access to other needed services.

- They could see others volunteering and participating in the care of the uninsured (the fellowship phenomenon).

- They could see their part in the full continuum of care.

Lesson 3: Intervening with the assignment and use of a medical home resulted in increased primary care, cost-effective care, reduced emergency room use, and reduced inpatient/specialty care.

Lesson 4: It is difficult to engage low income patients with chronic conditions or frequent emergency room users in disease management programs; however, for those we did engage, primary care use was increased by 100%.

Lesson 5: Care management, which was provided to all VODI enrollees, and disease management, which was provided as an additional intervention to VODI enrollees with a chronic illness or high-risk behavior, had an additive impact.

Lesson 6: Specifically managing high-risk and chronically ill patients with a Disease Management Program is an essential part of organizing health care and the delivery, and it is a critical component in providing effective care to an uninsured population.

Lesson 7: Strengthening linkages with community support systems and social services improves primary care use.

- The lessons learned and the work of building a community to care for the uninsured, are only the first steps. Because the demonstration project has been a success, there is a duty to go further. The next step is to tell other communities and the country what we have learned and to move our own community beyond the demonstration phase—which is now serving more than 33,000 people—to a system that can care for all the uninsured. However, local communities cannot do this alone. They must work in concert with our federal government partners to achieve care for all. In this respect, VODI must continue to collaborate, coordinate, organize coverage, and organize care for the uninsured in our community. Our collective hope is that soon national reform will take hold and embrace and partner with the efforts of local communities doing their best for those in most need.

Next Steps

Collaboration

Since its inception, VODI has been a driving force in amassing resources to serve the health care needs of the uninsured and underinsured population in Detroit. VODI was implemented with the notion that improving health care for the underserved requires community involvement, cultural sensitivity, greater knowledge of the underserved population, and a better understanding of how care is delivered in order to determine how care should be delivered in the future.

VODI's accomplishments demonstrate that such an approach can produce tangible improvements in service delivery and administrative processes and provide new information to address the health care needs of the uninsured and underinsured. VODI is building on this successful start and has now incorporated in Michigan as a nonprofit membership corporation with 501(c)(3) tax-exempt status. The formation of the nonprofit corporate entity was required for two reasons: First, VODI was limited to the geographic boundaries of the city of Detroit and Wayne County. The inclusion of providers and uninsured people outside the city is central to the region's ongoing economic viability and sustainability. The incorporation of VODI achieves these purposes while leaving the organization and its Detroit focus intact. Second, in order for VODI to function in a manner that complies with the Health Insurance Portability and Accountability Act (HIPAA), a legal entity is required to function as a clearinghouse and enter into formal legal contracts. VODI now has the proper legal basis for entering into such agreements.

In addition to changing its legal structure, VODI has collaborated on the development of aligned charity care policy guidelines among its partners. In the winter of 2005, VODI's Executive Committee supported the elements of the partners' charity care guidelines and agreed to create a uniform charity care policy in alignment with them. The major elements of the charity care policy are as follows:

- Use of the federal poverty level guidelines—all hospital-based facility services will be discounted at 100% for patients with incomes below 200% of the federal poverty level.

- Patients with incomes at or above 200% of the federal poverty level will receive a sliding fee scale discount on hospital services.

- Partners agreed to use VODI as the exclusive repository for their uninsured patient enrollment and utilization data.

- Federally Qualified Health Centers (FQHCs) agreed to continue to use sliding fee scales for their services.

Coordination

VODI and all of its partners played a major role in the success of the Detroit Health Care Stabilization Work Group. This work group, convened by Michigan governor Jennifer Granholm, was staffed by volunteer committees. Two of these committees were chaired by VODI Executive Committee members, and all committees had VODI representation. The chair of the Design and Staff Committee was Gail Warden, one of the original VODI CEO founders. VODI's executive director, as well as VODI partner CEOs, served on the Stabilization Task Force.

The work group recommended the establishment of the Detroit–Wayne County Health Authority. This authority was established in December 2003 with the approval of the Mayor of Detroit, the Wayne County Executive, and the Governor. Most credit VODI's work as the reason the work group was able to move forward at unprecedented pace. The work group incorporated many of VODI's best practices, concepts and infrastructures in their recommendations. These recommendations are providing the foundation for systemic change in Detroit, Wayne County and the southeast region of Michigan. The establishment of the authority is a bold extension of the work that the VODI consortium has been pursuing for the previous five years.

VODI is coordinating new grant opportunities with its partners and the Detroit–Wayne County Health Authority. A central challenge confronting the safety net system is the absence of an integrated medical record system for the uninsured network across the myriad of coordinated health providers in the county and region. Therefore, VODI has begun working to develop information technology systems that will improve the coordination of care for the uninsured and Medicaid recipients. In 2005, VODI received a Health Resources and Services Administration grant under the Healthy Community Access Program to develop the Integrated Minimum Clinic Record and Care Management Project. The purpose of this project is to expand access to primary health care and to improve the quality and management of chronic diseases for the medically uninsured in Wayne County. This will be accomplished by creating an integrated minimum clinical record system and expanding VODI's Care Management Program. The project will add health service information (e.g., dates of emergency department visits, diagnostic tests, and medications) to standard VODI patient record information. This information will be shared among all VODI network sites (FQHCs, look-alikes, community providers, and emergency departments) to improve the quality and coordination of care and to avoid the duplication of services.

The next steps for VODI include the engagement of its collaborative network of health providers, consumers, and advocates to extend the inclusiveness and effectiveness of the provider care network. VODI is using its expertise in organizing and managing a collaborative mechanism for planning, development, review, and submission of applications for FQHCs. The Health Resources and Services Administration continues to recognize VODI's vital role in coordinating this planning process in Detroit–Wayne County. As a result of VODI's coordination, two additional FQHCs and FQHC look-alike organizations have been approved, with two under review for approval at the time of the writing of this book.

Future efforts include identifying community health care providers that are interested in serving low-income uninsured persons, organizing community practitioners, managing specialty referrals based on provider specifications, and developing referral arrangements. One such effort will develop a community clinic affiliated with FQHC partners that will provide specialty and general dentistry care on the campus of Wayne County Community College when the University of Detroit Mercy leaves campus in 2008. The clinic will have 10–12 dental chairs, as well as dental residents, dentists, dental specialists, and dental specialty residence. The specialty dental clinic will operate based on need in the areas of pediatric dentistry, oral surgery, dentures, root canal, and periodontal care.

The future also includes ongoing reports based on VODI data. VODI will carry out the following activities:

- Trending reports on de-identified data (personal data) to aid in determining health trends and treatment responses based on historical data

- National norms comparison reports on primary care, emergency department, and specialty care utilization for the VODI population

- Data analyses related to repeat visit patterns

- Monitoring reports of care provided to the uninsured over time, documenting care to the uninsured, linking care with the demographics of the uninsured, and valuing care to the uninsured

- Information and documentation of the use pattern of the uninsured population over time—these utilization data have value not only for statistical research but also for the management of care to the uninsured and policy development

- Efforts to allow an electronic Medicaid application to be developed and the use of presumptive eligibility to improve timely enrollment

- Continue to identify and enroll eligible persons without health insurance into public insurance programs

VODI and its university partners will continue to demonstrate best practices for services delivered in low-income communities. VODI has established partnerships with Wayne State University's Eugene Applebaum College of Pharmacy and Health Sciences and School of Nursing; the University of Michigan's School of Dentistry, School of Social Work, and College of Pharmacy; and the University of Detroit's Mercy School of Nursing and Dentistry. These partnerships range from training pharmacists, to conducting brief interventions, to encouraging smokers to quit smoking, as well as fostering the use of cost-effective pharmaceutical therapies interventions, oral health disparities research, and telephonic blood pressure screening research, in addition to advisory board membership for a nurse-managed clinic. VODI's partnerships provide best practice applications for urban, low-income populations. In these projects, VODI's roles are

- To serve as a community-based partner helping to design and apply best practices

- To identify a research agenda from the perspective of the community and policy makers toward improving care for the uninsured

- To identify gaps in active research projects in Detroit–Wayne County and consider community needs when developing a plan for action

In partnership with the University of Michigan's Detroit Health Services Research Initiative, VODI hosted a conference on "Community-Based Research in Action: Agenda for the Future." Opportunities for research partnerships with the University of Michigan's schools and colleges were discussed, in addition to resources for applying for a variety of grants. As result of this conference, the University of Michigan School of Social Work is involved in a university-funded depression screening project, with VODI as its community research partner.

Organization of Coverage

Information system enhancements that facilitate coverage organization include a single electronic enrollment process integrated with the clinical information system. The expansion of the VODI collaborative has brought with it new opportunities to include information on public program patients, thus making VODI a central repository for information on the uninsured and public program patients seen within the care network.

The limited capacity of our collaborative network to provide primary care medical home coverage for all 200,000 uninsured in Detroit has also created some challenges. Thus, our next step in organizing coverage is to develop criteria for medical home assignment. These criteria are based on high utilizers (emergency room and inpatient) with three or more visits to an emergency room during a one-year time period and those with an inpatient stay or use of specialty care services so as to prioritize medical home assignments.

In addition, we will begin tracking medical home assignment and use in the database. Data collection and analysis are necessary to design coverage programs that promote prevention, improve health disparities, and determine the effectiveness of coverage programs.

Organization of the Care Delivery System

The Shared Minimum Clinical Electronic Medical Recorder System is not only a coordinating function it is also a function of organizing the care and delivery system. It will provide an opportunity to help FQHCs develop shared information using the same system clinic practice system, with specialty care referral components, practice management, scheduling, billing, and interfaces. It will also inform clinic and work flow efficiencies, accessible information for standard reports to the Health Resources and Services Administration, and administrative processes.

The fact that only 4.8% ($N = 130$) of enrollees agreed to participate in the Disease Management Program reflects the difficulty of trying to reach this population and the considerable amount of effort that is required to enroll them. As a result, a 24-Hour to 48-Hour Turnaround Program attempts to reach clients within 24–48 hours after their release from the emergency room, provided that they were not hospitalized. Efforts are then made to set up appointments for follow-up care with a primary care provider. The supposition is that more ideal utilization patterns may be promoted by directly establishing clients with a primary care medical home and educating them about the proper navigation of the health care system.

Policy Recommendations

VODI built a community collaborative that designed and coordinated activities to improve coverage and care for the uninsured in Detroit. The project significantly enhanced primary care use, reduced emergency room and inpatient/specialty care use, and reduced costs of enrollees. This was achieved through the local health care provider community collaboration on a set of actions related to care for the uninsured and through the coordination of those activities around the provision and integration of appropriate coverage and care services. A key design feature is that coverage and care were organized with a focus on primary care medical home assignment and *use*.

The VODI demonstration project designed and built a coverage and care mechanism for the uninsured. The project did not address alternative financing mechanisms. Chapters 3, 4, and 5 demonstrated that if a financing mechanism is in place (VODI used a voluntary mechanism) and coverage and care are organized, the pattern of care can be changed to improve access and quality while reducing costs. These findings have implications for designing policies that provide universal coverage to the uninsured.

The policy recommendations outlined here are derived from specific lessons learned from the VODI demonstration project. The VODI experience leads us to the conclusion that policy change is more likely and sustainable when the change advocated is a workable consensus of many different interests.

The problem of providing care for the uninsured is not simply an abstract problem. People's lives are at risk. The personal stories throughout this book demonstrate how the lack of insurance and health care can be devastating. As communities and safety net providers grapple with how to provide care to uninsured residents today, policy recommendations must focus on what help can be offered right now.

Policy Recommendation: Support Community Initiatives for the Uninsured

Building collaboration and commitment and working together in a common effort are the two most difficult—but also the most critical—aspects of the four components of the VODI Intervention Model. The VODI experience demonstrates the vital role that private foundation and government resources play in starting and sustaining a collaborative. Without the initial grant from the W. K. Kellogg Foundation, as well as the Community Access Program and Healthy Community Access Program grants and support from Ascension Health, the collaborative in Detroit could not have succeeded. The multiyear commitment represented by these funds provided a sustained base on which agreements and action could occur. A stronger local community collaboration and coordination effort produces stronger coverage and care, which, in turn, improves access, quality, and cost outcomes for tens of thousands of people.

Public and private funds should be allocated to community collaboratives that organize coverage and care for the uninsured. Policies and programs should focus on building collaborative capacity in communities and should include clear performance metrics to assess a community's leadership, structure, resources, potential for agreement, and capacity to provide coverage and care for the uninsured. Communities with inadequate capacity should be eligible for community capacity grants, in addition to community collaboration grants.

The core of a demonstration project is action. The VODI project demonstrates that action requires agreement, responsibility, accountability, and transparency. Information about what partners will do—and whether they in fact follow through—is essential for building coordinated systems for the uninsured. Information exchange is vital to successful coordination. This is an area in which goal articulation and progress toward meeting goals should be measured and reported.

Federal and state governments should work together to fund community scorecards that assess the goals and achievements of efforts to provide coverage and care for the uninsured. The allocation of federal and state funds should be driven by scorecard reporting and achievement. As a vehicle for building community scorecards, governments must invest in information exchange mechanisms, such as regional health information organizations, that move information across health care providers and payers. Information exchange is primarily a consensus-building effort; it is not simply a technical problem. Information exchange requires a community-wide workable consensus. Resources and community leadership are required if information exchange is to be effective.

Community scorecard development requires national, state, and local participation. Federal and state governments must work to build a consensus on scorecard metrics and elements. National and state standards must be outlined for each scorecard element that includes not only utilization and cost measures but outcomes relative to quality of care. Community collaboratives must be responsible for setting and achieving goals for each element of the scorecard. Federal and state governments must not only monitor community goals but also fund communities that successfully reach their targets. Figure 6.1 presents a sample community scorecard.

Figure 6.1. Sample Community Scorecard

The health care activities of each community should be tracked in nine areas. A community collaborative board of directors should set goals in each of the following areas.

Target Population: Community's Uninsured = _____
　　Enrollment (share of uninsured enrolled)
　　Number of established enrollees, new enrollees, Medicaid eligible
　　Number of uninsured enrollees, screened and transferred to insurance

---

Consumer Profile
　　Demographic characteristics
　　Satisfaction with enrollment and care

Resources for Target Population
　　Number of network access points for preventive care, primary
　　care, diagnostic/laboratory work, pharmacy, and acute care
　　Number of specialty, emergency, and inpatient care
　　providers linked to primary care centers

Figure 6.1. Sample Community Scorecard (Continued)

Enhanced Funding/Medicaid Match Funds
    Federal grants and earmarks
    State, county, city funds
    Health system funds
    Foundation grants

Utilization of Network Services (compare to Centers for
Disease Control and published guidelines)
    Medical home visits, preventive care visits, primary care visits, diagnostic/
    laboratory services, pharmacy, specialty visits, emergency room visits,
    acute care visits, inpatient admissions, and average length of stay

Efficiency
    Reduced emergency room usage (visit/enrollee), rate of
    preventable hospitalizations and emergency room visits,
    effective tracking (percentage of care tracked)

Cost-Effectiveness (measured using four benchmarks)
    Benchmark for physician costs
    University Hospital Consortium for facility costs
    Medicaid cost for types of service
    Medicare benchmark for Medicaid payment

Network Financial Viability
    Revenues for care of target population
    Operating profit or loss on enrolled population
    Safety net provider payer balance between Medicaid, Medicare,
    commercial insurance, and uninsured (uncompensated care)
    Charity care (measured with standard community-wide metric)

Quality Measurements
(Healthcare Effectiveness Data and Information Set)
    Number of immunizations; frequency of diabetes tests, screening for diabetes,
    hypertension, and asthma; number of cancer screenings; prenatal/postpartum
    care; surveys on patient's experience; number of well visits; preventable emergency
    room and hospital admissions; and frequency of selected procedures performed

Policy Recommendation: Universal Coverage and Care

Building a universal coverage system, such as expanded Medicare, is a top policy priority. The Institute of Medicine has summarized the primary barrier to a policy that would provide health insurance for everybody:

> Present-day efforts to reduce or eliminate uninsurance build on nearly a century of campaigns to bring about universal health insurance coverage. Past campaigns have yielded both incremental changes and major reforms but not universal coverage due to the challenge to major contractual changes posed by American political arrangements and the lack of political leadership strong and sustained enough to forge a workable consensus of coverage legislation[1].

The experience in Detroit demonstrates that when sustained leadership builds a workable consensus, coverage and care for the uninsured can be changed. The Detroit consensus used a voluntary financing mechanism to organize and provide coverage and care to a defined uninsured population. Much of the health insurance debate has centered on the financing mechanism that should be used to provide universal coverage. The use of a voluntary financing mechanism in Detroit highlights the need for a permanent financing mechanism. VODI does not provide information that would recommend a specific source or type of financing. However, VODI does demonstrate that having a financing mechanism is vital to organizing coverage and care for the uninsured.

One manifestation of the lack in universal coverage is that information on insurance coverage is not coordinated between the private and the public insurance systems. It is possible, but difficult, to identify who has insurance and who may be eligible for public or private insurance. VODI enrollment workers worked very hard to assist clients in securing insurance and getting needed care. The value of organizing coverage is diminished if there is no organized delivery system to provide the full continuum of care to uninsured clients. The performance of health insurance plans in facilitating a regular and continuing care relationship for enrollees through medical home assignment and use should be a key factor in the design of any health insurance coverage plan.

A coverage system that does not have access to an organized care delivery system is only a partial solution. Providing universal health insurance without simultaneously organizing the delivery system cannot achieve the objective of facilitating appropriate care utilization patterns or cost-effective

---

1.   Committee on Consequences of Uninsurance,   Insuring America's Health: Principles and Recommendations, P. 3 (Washington D.C.:National Academy Press, 2004)

care in the United States. A continuing relationship with a primary care provider with a support system of care, as well as associated care and disease management, is the hallmark of an organized delivery system. Access to and use of a regular source of primary care and preventive services are the key factors in the design of any effective health care system. Primary care cannot stand alone; it must be formally linked to the continuum of care.

National universal health insurance should contain all four elements of the VODI Intervention Model: collaboration, coordination, coverage, and care. Table 6.1 demonstrates that current insurance mechanisms do not currently incorporate all four elements. The path to health care reform requires steps toward implementing change in each of the eight cells that make each a row in the table.

Table 6.1. VODI Intervention Model (VIM) Insurance Assessment Table

	Collaboration/ Coordination	Coverage			Care			
	Workable Consensus (National/Local)	Finance	Eligibility	Benefits	Medical Home		Disease/ Care Manage-ment	Access to the Continuum of Care
					Assign-ment	Use		
VODI	X	X	X	X	X	X	X	X
Medicaid	X	X	X	X	X			X
Medicare Part A & B	X	X	X	X				X
FFS Commercial Insurance		X	X	X			X	X
Commercial HMO/PPO		X	X	X	X		X	X

X = Element is Present

Universal health care is primarily a national issue. The debate has largely centered on who should pay and what financing mechanisms should be used, rather than how we can create local collaboration and coordination of services and organize the coverage and care delivery systems for continuous improvement in community health status. Although a financing mechanism can be constructed nationally, care is delivered locally. A national health insurance policy that ignores local delivery challenges and capacities will inevitably fail. A local workable consensus is required to implement any national universal health care policy.

While leaders are working toward universal coverage, additional policy initiatives can and should be taken. For example, a National Uninsured Coverage and Care System should be built. Such a system could be built in four incremental steps. First, coverage information should be coordinated across public and private systems so that providers know who is uninsured. This system should integrate Medicaid outreach programs with efforts to identify the uninsured. Coordinated insurance should be available to communities that are organizing coverage for the uninsured. Second, state innovation must be encouraged. State coverage initiatives such as employer mandates or expanded Medicaid plans (e.g., Dirigo Health plan in Maine) should be encouraged through the promulgation of more flexible Medicaid and ERISA (Employee Retirement Income Security Act) rules. Third, funds allocated for uninsured patients (either disproportionate share funds or charity care tax expenditures) should be linked to the care of identified uninsured patients. And finally, all identified uninsured patients should be assigned a medical home.

The establishment of National Uninsured Coverage and Care System and the implementation of the community initiatives outlined here would create a national policy for the uninsured even without national health insurance. These two recommendations have the potential to produce large changes within the framework of a workable consensus.

Policy Recommendation: Fund Primary Care That Is Linked to the Continuum of Care

Assignment and use of a medical home is certainly the first step in bringing an uninsured person into the health care system. However, care cannot stop at the medical home. In some cases, specialty and hospital care may be required. A link between primary care providers and health systems that provide emergency, specialty, and inpatient care was successfully implemented by VODI. The link between FQHCs and health systems was used to provide the continuum of care for uninsured VODI registrants. Building care networks requires collaboration and coordination among partners. VODI clearly demonstrates the value of having a medical home in reducing emergency room use, as well as inpatient/specialty care use.

One of the best ways to do so is to expand FQHC funding. Federal and state FQHC funding through Medicaid Cost Based Reimbursement payments for primary care should also be increased. Policy makers should make the emergency room a last resort for the uninsured, not the only place that is legally required to serve uninsured. A variety of additional incentives are needed to link private doctors to uninsured care networks and to encourage the use of disease management programs for subpopulations of the uninsured. The integration of disease prevention services with primary care for the uninsured is a high priority. Because care management and disease management are additive, primary care funding must explicitly and directly fund these activities.

The expansion and uninterrupted linkage of pharmacy services with primary care is a critical policy step toward improving health status, decreasing emergency room utilization, reducing preventable hospitalization, and reducing the costs of care. The federal government's 340B program should be expanded and made available to all safety net providers that link primary and specialty care for the uninsured. More uniform programs including "Share the Care" programs implemented by pharmacies, such as the one at the Detroit Health Department (described in Chapters 2 and 4) should also be readily linked to safety net primary care providers.

Policy Recommendation: Fund Specialty Care that helps Link the Continuum of Care

Although the U.S. government funds health care services for the medically-underserved for public health, health promotion and preventive services through the Centers for Disease Control and Prevention (CDC), and State and local health departments, primary care services through FQHC funding, tertiary care using Disproportionate Share Hospital (DSH) dollars, and pharmacy services using 340B funding, there is no funding mechanism for secondary or specialty care for the uninsured. Although the above funding sources are currently a long way from adequately covering this country's underserved and uninsured they are critical resources toward helping to fill a broadening gap in services for the uninsured. However there is no funding source earmarked to specifically pay for basic secondary care services for underserved and uninsured populations, such as paying to see a specialist like a cardiologist or a general surgeon for common medical problems, or paying for basic diagnostic studies such as an ultrasound or cardiac stress test[2]. VODI found that providing and therefore adding specialty care services to primary care and pharmacy services was also a key policy step toward improving health status, decreasing emergency room utilization, reducing preventable hospitalization, and reducing the costs of care. We recommend developing a specialty care funding pool by enhancing targeted FQHC

---

2.   Committee on the Consequences of Uninsurance, Insuring America's Health: Principles and Recommendations. (Washington D.C.: National Academy Press, 2004)

grant funding and enhanced FQHC Medicaid cost based reimbursement payments as the vehicle to pay for specialty care funding.

VODI clearly demonstrates the cost-saving potential of organizing coverage and care for the uninsured. Governments must invest in organized delivery systems that enhance access, incentivise appropriate care utilization and manage care for the uninsured if health status improvement and cost savings are to be achieved.

Policy Recommendation: Organize Charity Care

Currently, health care for the uninsured is paid for by government subsidy (including funding for public health departments, FQHC funding, cost based reimbursement, 340B pharmacy programs, and Disproportionate Share Hospital (DSH) payments) and charity care, which is paid for by providers. The financing mechanism for the VODI project was voluntary. As a part of that financing mechanism VODI spent a lot of upfront time identifying, cataloging, coordinating and optimizing the full use of our current local government and charity care resources. Given this, providers agreed to provide care to VODI enrollees without assurance of direct payment, because they believed that an investment in better organizing the delivery system—and getting people connected to primary care providers and out of emergency rooms and hospitals—would decrease their overall uncompensated care costs, improve health outcomes, and provide a community benefit, which it did. Because the VODI partners were nonprofit organizations, this activity was a part of their charitable contribution to the community.

Hospitals receive a tax exemption, as nonprofit entities under the IRS 501(c) (3). In exchange for this tax exempt status hospitals are required to provide an annual report on the community benefit they provide[3]. An element of this community benefit is providing care to those without insurance, such as the use of charity care funds.[4] However the system of reporting and counting of charity care is very complex. Some calculations are based on charges, others on cost. Charity care does not include bad debt

---

3.   Community benefits are programs or activities that provide treatment and/or promote health and healing as a response to identified community needs. They are not provided for marketing purposes. A community benefit must meet at least one of the following criteria: 1. generates a low or negative margin, 2. responds to the needs of special populations such as minorities, older persons, and persons with disabilities who are living in poverty, 3. Supplies services or programs that would likely be discontinued- or would need to be provided by another non-for-profit or government provider-if the decision was made on a purely financial basis, 4. Response to public health needs, and 5. Involves education or research that improves overall community health. Source: Catholic Health Association, "A Guide for Planning and Reporting Community Benefit, 2006. CHA, St. Louis, Mo.

4.   Charity Care are services provided for which hospitals neither receive nor prospectively expect to receive payment based on the patients inability to pay. Charity care does not include bad debt and is a component of the Community Benefit standard.

and bad debt[5] is not included as a part of the community benefit standard but is usually tracked, recorded, and quantified by hospitals.

Though it is clear that nonprofit organizations receive a substantial tax break because they provide a community benefit by caring for the uninsured, there is no standard for how much care should be delivered as part of that obligation. Not only is there no standard, but there is also no uniform metric. The absence of a clear standard means that the level of charity care an institution gives is largely a function of the commitment of that organization's leadership, the hospital's mission, the hospital's financial condition and/or business practices, community needs and other factors.

Until a solution is found for universal coverage and care for this country, hospital charity care will continue to be all that stands between our country's current policy dilemma and an access crisis for millions of Americans.[6]

If government subsidies and charity care are going to be used to finance care for the uninsured, then several changes are necessary. A clear uniform calculation and reporting standard for charity care should be promulgated with an external financial reporting requirement to list charity care as an individual expense item to increase the transparency of this benefit. Government subsidies should be coordinated to ensure adequate coverage for the uninsured. Subsidies and charity care should be tied directly to the cost of care that each provider gives to uninsured patients. Additionally government subsidies should be coordinated to ensure adequate coverage and access to the full continuum of care with incentives that promote primary care as the focal point of care for those without health insurance. Charity care and subsidies must link coverage and care, as outlined in the VODI Intervention Model. Tax exemptions and government subsidies must be targeted to an organized system of care for uninsured individuals. In fact, charity care should adhere to the elements for insurance outlined in Table 6.1. And finally, the impact of many of the community-benefit activities provided by health care organizations are not readily measurable or quantifiable and therefore difficult to assess their full impact. We must come up with creative methodologies that do provide measurable impact assessments or at least measurable associations between community benefit activities and positive health outcomes in local communities.

Federal and state regulations and financing mechanisms must encourage the kind of collaboration and coordination that proved so effective in Detroit. Charity care for the uninsured can be made more cost-effective.

---

5. Bad debts are services for which hospitals billed for and anticipated reimbursement but did not receive payment. Bad debt is not included as a part of the Community Benefit standard.
6. American Hospital Association. Testimony of the AHA before the U.S. Senate Committee on Finance. Taking the pulse of Charitable Care and Community Benefits at Nonprofit Hospitals. September 13, 2006.

The patterns of care promoted by the VODI Intervention Model were cost-effective. Chapter 4 showed that medical home use reduced emergency room and inpatient/specialty care use. Patients who transitioned from emergency to primary care also used emergency room services less. The VODI partners were correct: Organizing charity care did result in cost savings. Chapter 4 calculated significant savings from medical home use, less frequent emergency room use, and transitions from emergency to primary care. These savings resulted from changing care patterns and from the coordination of charity care among VODI's partners.

Community Choices

The path to taking care of the uninsured goes through every community in America. No community is spared. The choice then for each community becomes whether to take action or remain inactive, hoping the problem will just go away or someone else will solve it. Inaction has significant economic and health consequences for local communities and for the uninsured. The current situation is unsustainable. The experience in Detroit demonstrates that proactive collaborative action with coordination of the delivery system can facilitate organizing coverage and care, and therefore improve care for the uninsured in a cost effective manner. The challenge for each community is that first the leadership must come together and acknowledge a local need for change. Using workable solutions derived from the steps of collaboration, coordination, coverage and care, as outlined in this book, every community will build a success story for *taking care of the uninsured* and chart their own *path to health care reform*.

Appendix A

Detroit Community Profile

The VODI project took place in Detroit, which provided a unique community context. We provide this community profile to help readers understand the context of the VODI intervention so they can make comparisons to their own communities.

The VODI project did not occur in a vacuum—it occurred in a *community*. One strong motivation for providers to participate in this demonstration was the deteriorating environment for providing health care in Detroit: The city has experienced a high concentration of uninsured residents, an under funded safety net system, an erosion of safety net providers, and poor health outcomes.

In Michigan, 25% of the uninsured live below 100% of the federal poverty level for a family of three ($16,600 per year), 63% live below 200% of the federal poverty level ($33,200 per year), and 85% live below 300% of the federal poverty level ($49,800 per year). About one-third of Detroit's population is dependent on Medicaid, and one-fifth of the population—approximately 200,000 people—is uninsured.

Age-adjusted death rates for heart disease, stroke, cancer, and even diseases that are more amenable to treatment, such as pneumonia, are higher in Detroit than in Michigan and in most other large American cities (see Table 1.2). The City of Detroit Health Department monitors "sentinel death rates," which represent deaths from conditions resulting from the failure of primary care, lifestyle or environmental factors, or the lack of access to available treatment. Collectively, sentinel deaths have been rising in Detroit over the last decade, indicating that health care infrastructure in Detroit is being challenged to meet the most basic needs of its residents. Detroit area seniors age 60-74 are dying at a rate 48% higher, with hospitalization rates 37% higher than their peers in the rest of Michigan, another indicator of primary care resource deficits.[1]

Table 1.2. Age-Adjusted Death Rates from Selected Causes, 2005

Cause of Death	Death Rate (per 100,000)		
	U.S.	Michigan	Detroit
Heart disease	240.8	263.9	401.1
Cancer	193.5	197.6	235.7
Stroke	56.2	57.4	66.2
Diabetes	25.4	27.5	36.6
Influenza/pneumonia	22.6	20.1	24.8

These adverse health outcomes have been accompanied by social factors that are known to be associated with illness and premature death, including poverty, unemployment, incomplete education, teenage pregnancy, substance abuse, and inadequate health insurance coverage—all of which are overrepresented among Detroit residents. Collectively, the social and health status indicators in Detroit are about 40% worse than those in both the state and the nation.

A number of barriers to care have produced adverse outcomes. The first barrier is the lack of health insurance in Detroit. Only 35% of Detroit's residents have commercial insurance, compared to 63% statewide.[2] Other financial barriers include lack of appropriate transportation resources and childcare.

The shortage of primary care physicians in Detroit is another barrier. Roughly 60% of primary care physicians have left the city since 1997, and 60% of the city has been designated by the federal government as medically underserved. The city has a primary capacity to serve approximately 48,000 of those without insurance, leaving more than 150,000 uninsured without access to any primary care. According to the Robert Wood Johnson Foundation's Urgent Matters analysis of ten U.S. communities, Wayne County faces a significant shortage of primary care physicians, with a rate

---

1.   Lee Kallenbach, Herbert C. Smitherman, Jr.,*Dying Before Their Time: The startling truth about mortality and Detroit area seniors*, report prepared for the Detroit Area Agency on Aging, 2002.
2.   Detroit Health Care Stabilization Workgroup, "Strengthening the Safety Net in Detroit and Wayne County."

of only 147.3 primary care physicians per 100,000. The lowest rate in the country is 6.6 per 100,000 in Spotsylvan County, VA, and the highest is 694.1 primary care physicians per 100,000 population in Falls Church,VA.[3] This dearth of access to basic primary care costs the major Detroit–Wayne County health systems nearly $350 million annually in uncompensated care predominantly due to high emergency room and preventable hospitalization use rates.[4]

Another significant barrier to care in Detroit, however, is the city's under funded safety net system. In 2001, Michigan had the lowest Medicaid health plan capitation rate in the country. The Urban Institute estimated that the statewide per member, per month Medicaid rate for 2001 was $105.35. Thus, Michigan's rate was almost 50% lower than the national/state median rate of $150.60. The highest rate in the country was $209.34, nearly double Michigan's rate and 69% higher than the Medicare managed care rate for the state. Michigan increased its capitation rates in 2003, but it is likely that the state's rates remain below those paid by other states.[5]

- The estimated shortfall in funding for the provision of care to Medicaid and low-income uninsured populations in Wayne County was estimated by Michigan Governor Jennifer Granholm's Safety Net Stabilization Work Group to be $300 million.

The chronic under funding of Medicaid, cuts imposed by the Balance Budget Act of 1997, declining investment income, the loss of commercial payments, and the concentration of Medicaid recipients in Detroit have combined to result in declining financial margins for Detroit health care providers. This is compounded by the fact that Detroit has no public hospital nor a local funding mechanism for indigent care. Data show that Detroit hospitals had worse margins than their counterparts in Michigan in 2001. Patient margin is the percentage difference between net patient revenue and total expenses. In that year, Detroit hospitals were paid nearly 8% less than their expenses, compared to roughly 3% in other areas of the state. In other communities with higher commercial payer mix and healthier populations, providers are better able to cope with this chronic under funding.[6]

As a result of underpayment, several Wayne County–based, Medicaid-qualified health plans have been placed under state supervision in order to continue operation. The largest Medicaid health plan in Wayne County

---

3. Urgent Matters, Robert Wood Johnson Foundation and George Washington University Medical Center, School of Public Health and Health Services Department of Health Policy, March 2004.
4. Detroit Health Care Stabilization Work Group, "Strengthening the Safety Net in Detroit and Wayne County."
5. Stabilization Report *opcit*
6. Stabalization Report *opcit*

went out of business after being placed under state supervision. In 2002, the county's largest Medicaid delivery system received a $50 million bridge payment from the state, county, and city in order to continue services at two of its major safety net hospitals.

The under funding of health care has produced a system that is both inefficient and unsustainable. Investing in chronic disease care management is impossible in an under funded system, despite overwhelming evidence that such management is cost-effective. Physician lost, clinic and hospital closures, and financial losses provide clear evidence of the lack of sustainability of the current system. Examples of inefficiencies include the overuse of emergency rooms and the lack of coordinated care for resource-limited patients.

In summary, Detroit–Wayne County has seen increasing numbers of uninsured, rising numbers of Medicaid recipients, and decreasing numbers of primary care physicians. Health care costs have risen secondary to increasing levels of unmanaged chronic illness, high preventable hospitalization rates and unnecessary emergency room use rates, with health status decreasing.

Appendix B

Statistical and Epidemiological Appendix

Cohort Studies

An important part of evaluating a project or conducting research is looking at the factors associated with an outcome of interest. Because this book is interested in the effects that variables had on the utilization and coverage patterns of the uninsured, some logical outcomes of interest are based on a categorization of certain utilization and coverage patterns as consistent or not consistent with the objectives of the VODI Intervention Model. With those outcomes defined, a number of analyses may look at which factors are associated with them.

This evaluation may be considered a retrospective cohort study. The evaluation is a type of cohort study because participants were categorized on the basis of their exposures and then occurrences of the outcomes of interest were determined. It is a retrospective cohort, as opposed to a prospective cohort study, because both the outcomes and exposures were present before the evaluation was carried out. The exposures could be determined because data were collected during the process of the VODI project. Prospective cohort studies, on the other hand, involve the selection of subjects and the determination of exposure at the initiation of the study, but the outcome of interest is not yet present before the evaluation is started. The subjects are then followed over time to see whether they develop the outcome or disease of interest.[1]

---

1.   Charles H. Hennekens and Julie E. Buring. *Epidemiology in Medicine* (Boston: Little, Brown, 1987).

Measures of Association

"Measures of association" are epidemiological calculations that are used to determine whether a significant relationship exists between two factors. Two such measures of association are the odds ratio and relative risk, both of which estimate the strength of the relationship between the event (or outcome) and the exposure of interest.[2] Which of these two measures is selected depends on the type of study that is being conducted. Some types of studies permit the calculation of the incidence of an outcome (or disease), whereas other study types do not.[3] For cohort studies (both prospective and retrospective), relative risk, which is the ratio of the incidence in the exposed population (those who have a particular exposure of interest) compared to the incidence in the nonexposed population (those who do not have the exposure of interest), is the preferred measure of association.

Though relative risk is the preferred measure of association for cohort studies, the disadvantage of this measure is that it does not account for the effects of a third variable (in addition to the exposure and outcome variables) without some type of adjustment. This is an important point because a variable of interest may appear to be associated with the outcome, but that association may actually be attributable to that variable's association with a third variable—the actual factor related to the outcome. This situation is referred to as "positive confounding." Alternatively, a variable of interest may falsely appear to be unassociated with the outcome because of its relationship to a third variable, a phenomenon known as "negative confounding." Variables that cause positive or negative confounding are known collectively as "confounders."[4]

Because of the possible problems of confounding, the evaluation conducted for this book included another measure of association as a preliminary step. This measure, typically used in case-control studies, is known as the odds ratio. In contrast to the cohort study, a case-control study categorizes subjects on the basis of whether they have the outcome (or disease) of interest, and then investigators determine the presence or absence of the exposures.[5] Odds ratios were determined here using a statistical technique that is easily implemented with statistical software programs to look at the simultaneous effect of multiple variables.[6] This technique involves multivariate analysis and is discussed further in the next section of this appendix.

---

2.   National Center for Suicide Prevention Training, "Locating, Understanding and Presenting Youth Suicide Data," February 14, 2007, http://www.ncspt.org/courses/course1A-self/id137.htm.
3.   Hennekens and Buring, *Epidemiology in Medicine.*
4.   Ibid.
5.   Ibid.
6.   Paul D. Allison, *Logistic Regression Using the SAS System: Theory and Application* (Cary, NC: SAS Institute, 1999).

The odds ratio is relatively straightforward to understand and interpret. Paul Allison (1999) gives a definition of the odds of an outcome (or event) as "the ratio of the expected number of times that an event will occur to the expected number of times that it will not occur."[7]. For example, the odds that an enrollee who joined the VODI program before 2004 used services within the assigned network are roughly 1.26. This means that there are 1.26 times as many occurrences of post-registration, assigned network use as there are nonoccurrences (or no post-registration, assigned network use) among those enrolled before 2004.

The crude odds ratio is calculated by taking the odds of the exposed group and dividing it by the odds of the nonexposed group. This ratio is easily calculated with a two-by-two table, as Allison (1999) describes, by obtaining "the product of the two main diagonal frequencies" and then dividing it by "the product of the two off diagonal frequencies."[8] This is illustrated in the following table.

	Continuous Pattern (Event)	Not Continuous Pattern (Nonevent)
Female (exposed)	2,393	6,532
Male (nonexposed)	979	5,509

The odds ratio = (2393 x 5509) / (979 x 6532) = 2.0. In this example, the odds of women showing a "continuous pattern" are 2.0 times higher than the men's odds, or the odds of the women showing a continuous pattern are 100% higher than the men's odds. Alternatively, one could say that the women are 2.0 times more likely to use the service "continuously" than the men, as this finding is statistically significant.

If the odds ratio had not been statistically significant from 1.0, then no significant association between gender and the pattern of utilization would have been found. The statistical significance is determined by looking at the confidence interval for the odds ratio. If the confidence interval for the odds ratio includes 1.0, then the association is not statistically significant. The value of 1.0 for the odds ratio shows no association because, in that case, the odds of the outcome occurring among the exposed population are the same as the odds of the outcome occurring among the nonexposed population.[9]

---

7.   Ibid.
8.   Ibid.
9.   Hennekens and Buring, *Epidemiology in Medicine.*

The use of odds ratios to estimate relative risk for a cohort study, however, often results in biased estimates of relative risk when the event or outcome is not rare. The bias involves an overestimation of relative risk when the measure is greater than 1 and an underestimation when the measure is less than 1. Either of these biases may overstate the association between the outcome and the exposure.[10] Consequently, this evaluation applied a correction formula to the odds ratios to obtain less biased estimates of relative risk.

Multivariate Analysis

Multivariate regression analyses are frequently used to examine the effects of multiple explanatory variables on an outcome variable. (Explanatory variables include the exposures of interest and third variables with possible effects on the associations with the outcome.) The result is that the confounding effects are controlled for and adjusted estimates (estimates that have been adjusted to account for confounding) may be obtained.[11]

Logistic regression is a type of multivariate analysis for dependent variables that are categorical[12] (as opposed to multiple linear regressions, which have quantitative outcomes).[13] Logistic regression models were used to calculate odds ratios in this analysis. The results of the logistic regressions with the adjusted odds ratios are presented alongside the crude odds ratios (which have not been adjusted to account for confounding). This allows easy comparisons of the measures of association before and after the effects of confounding have been taken into account. Finally, the estimates of relative risk and confidence intervals are included after the correction formula presented by Zhang and Yu (1998)[14] has been applied.

A detailed discussion of the scientific theory behind the different types of regression models is beyond the scope of this book. However, a note is made that a multivariate regression model may be represented with equations showing the various constituents that determine it. The equation representing the logit model (logistic regression model) as denoted in Allison (1999) is presented here:

$$\text{Log } [p_i/1 - p_i] = \alpha + \beta_1 X_{i1} + \beta_2 X_{i2} + \ldots + \beta_k X_{ki}$$

---

10. Jun Zhang, and Kai F. Yu, "What's the Relative Risk? A Method of Correcting the Odds Ratio in Cohort Studies of Common Outcomes," *Journal of the American Medical Association* 280, no. 19 (1998): 1690–91.

11.   Allison, *Logistic Regression Using the SAS System.*

12.   Ibid.

13.   Glossary of Research Terms," February 14, 2007, http://www.msu.edu/unit/chmrsch/Resources/Glossary%20of%20Research%20Terms.doc..

14.   Zhang and Yu, "What's the Relative Risk?"

where *i* represents subject 1, subject 2....subject *n* (where subject *n* is the last subject included in the model); *k* is the number of explanatory variables; *pi* is the probability that *yi* = 1 (*yi* is the dependent variable for each individual in the model). An important point of interest is that the odds equal *p* / (1 – *p*); ∞ is the intercept; β represents the coefficient for the respective explanatory variable; and *X* denotes the explanatory variable (X_1 is the first explanatory variable included in the model, X_2 is the second, and so on, up to explanatory variable *Xk*).

A detailed explanation of how the maximum likelihood estimation works for this model and why logistic regression is preferred for categorical outcomes is not needed to understand the remainder of this appendix. For those interested in that information, Paul Allison's *Logistic Regression Using the SAS System: Theory and Application* provides a good resource.[15]

Fortunately, statistical software packages such as SAS, STATA, and SPSS can easily determine the coefficients for all of the explanatory variables and other relevant measures for the logistic regression model. The regression coefficients (calculated by exponentiating the regression coefficients) and their confidence intervals are also provided by these programs.[16] To run one of these models, specification of the proper dependent variable and the independent (explanatory) variables is necessary after they have been properly coded. When all explanatory variables (exposures and third variables) are included in the model, the coefficients and odds ratios produced control for all other independent variables in the model. However, the interpretation of the odds ratio remains the same, except that one can note the association while controlling for the other explanatory variables in the model.[17]

For example, one can consider the logistic regression model of the history of any within–assigned network utilization after registration (regardless of whether the pattern was continuous). For this model, the adjusted odds ratio of 1.57 for the association of gender and that outcome may be interpreted as follows: Females were 1.57 times more likely to have a history of any within–assigned network utilization than the males when controlling for place of enrollment, age, marital status, hours worked per week, total monthly household income, number of individuals in the household, and presence or absence of one or more of the qualifying chronic conditions (asthma, cancer, diabetes mellitus, and hypertension).

Notes about working with such large samples as seen in Chapters 3 and 4 should be made. With such large sample sizes, statistically significant

---

15. Allison, *Logistic Regression Using the SAS System.*
16. Aviva Petrie and Caroline Sabin, *Medical Statistics at a Glance,* 2nd ed. (Malden, MA: Blackwell, 2005).
17. Allison, *Logistic Regression Using the SAS System.*

results may be obtained even when a small difference is obtained.[18] However, the coefficients, which are used to calculate the odds ratios, are "consistent" when they are determined by the maximum likelihood method for the binary logit model (a type of logistic regression model). This consistency means that the coefficients (and odds ratios) have a greater probability of being "within some small distance of the true value" when the sample size gets larger.[19] Consequently, logistic regression through the maximum method provides an appropriate analytical technique.

The estimated relative risks and their confidence intervals, which are determined by applying the correction formula, may be interpreted in a similar manner. The formula for correcting the estimate obtained from the odds ratios is given by Zhang and Yu (1998) as follows:

$$RR = OR / [(1 - P0) + (P0 * OR)]$$

where *RR* denotes relative risk; *OR* represents the odds ratio; and P_0 is the incidence of the outcome in the nonexposed group.

The confidence intervals may also be corrected by using this formula on the upper and lower confidence limits.[20]

Similar to the odds ratio, relative risk shows a significant association when its confidence interval does not include 1.0. Relative risk can be explained in language similar to that used for the odds ratio. For example, the relative risk for the association between gender and the outcome of any post-enrollment service utilization is 1.24. This mean that females were 1.24 times as likely to show post-enrollment service utilization than males, whereas participants enrolled through the "other" type of enrollment site were less than half as likely to have used services after enrollment compared to those enrolled through a primary care site.[21]

While logistic regression models are appropriately used when the outcome is a dichotomous category, other methods are employed when the outcome takes on many different numeric values. For outcomes that involve continuous quantitative variables (those that may take on any numeric value), ordinary linear regression is often used.[22] Additionally, ordinary linear regression, in the past, was also applied to dependent variables involving counts of events.[23] However, count data involves nonnegative integer values to quantify the number of events. In this book, some of our dependent

---

18.   Hennekens and Buring, *Epidemiology in Medicine.*
19.   Allison, *Logistic Regression Using the SAS System.*
20.   Zhang and Yu, "What's the Relative Risk?"
21.   Hennekens and Buring, *Epidemiology in Medicine.*
22.   Glossary of Research Terms,"
23.   Allison, *Logistic Regression Using the SAS System.*

variables involved counts of the number of visits to a health care site. We did not use the ordinary linear regression methods in this book because our visit counts were not normally distributed. This lack of normality is a violation of one of the assumptions that must be met to carry out ordinary linear regression.[24] While the assumption technically requires that the residuals are normally distributed, utilization data has been noted as having residuals that show " a similar distribution to the original data."[25]

The Poisson regression is a method that was developed to handle the skewed distributions of count data.[26] [27]However, this regression has other assumptions that must be met. One assumption is that the standardized residuals are normally distributed. This assumption may not be met when a high proportion of zeros are present.[28] A second assumption is that the mean must be equal to the variance.[29]

If the first assumption is violated because of a high proportion of zeros, then a zero-inflated model may be a better choice.[30] The zero-inflated model is a two-part model that uses a logistic regression in the first part and a Poisson or negative binomial (another type of model for count data) in the second part.[31] The two parts allow the determination of explanatory variables that influence the probability of not making any visits (the zero values for our outcome) "over and above that expected from a usual Poisson model" and the determination of explanatory variables that influence the frequency or intensity of post-enrollment service utilization.[32]

Diehr (1999) discusses the advantages of using the one- or two-part models for health care utilization data. Diehr notes that one-part models have the advantage of simplicity. On the other hand, two-part models, such as the zero-inflated Poisson, have the advantage of providing a technique that may better suit the data and may lend more "insight into the utilization process."[33] To determine whether a two-part model is the more appropriate choice, a Vuong test statistic may be used. A Vuong test statistic that is

24. Petrie and Sabin, *Medical Statistics at a Glance*.
25. P. Diehr, D. Yanez, A. Ash, M. Hornbrook, and D. Y. Lin, "Methods for Analyzing Health Care Utilization and Costs," *Annual Review of Public Health* 20 (1999): 125–44.
26. Allison, *Logistic Regression Using the SAS System*.
27. Diehr et al., "Methods for Analyzing Health Care Utilization and Costs."
28. J. D. Lewsey, and W. M. Thomson, "The Utility of Zero-Inflated Poisson and Zero-Inflated Negative Binomial Models: A Case Study of Cross-Sectional and Longitudinal DMF Data Examining the Effect of Socio-Economic Status," *Community Dentistry and Oral Epidemiology* 32, no. 3 (June 2004): 183–89.
29. Allison, *Logistic Regression Using the SAS System*.
30. Lewsey and Thomson, "The Utility of Zero-Inflated Poisson and Zero-Inflated Negative Binomial Models."
31. Diehr et al., "Methods for Analyzing Health Care Utilization and Costs."
32. Lewsey and Thomson, "The Utility of Zero-Inflated Poisson and Zero-Inflated Negative Binomial Models."
33. Ibid.

higher than 1.96 indicates that the zero-inflated model will provide "a better fit" of the data.[34] We carried out a zero-inflated Poisson, as well as a one-part Poisson, to calculate a Vuong test statistic for the number of emergency room visits made during the first year after enrollment.

This outcome was examined because it had the highest percentage of zero counts. (Approximately 75% of active enrollees had no emergency room visits during their first year of participation.) We obtained a Vuong test statistic that was lower than 1.96; therefore, one-part models were used for all three outcomes modeled in Chapter 4.

When the second assumption is violated because the variance is greater than the mean, a phenomenon known as "overdispersion" results and standard errors for the regression coefficients may be underestimated. This underestimation may lead to the conclusion that an exposure variable has a statistically significant association when, in fact, it does not. Although overdispersion in a Poisson regression may be corrected using certain methods, an alternative method is negative binomial regression.[35]

We chose to run negative binomial regressions for our analyses in Chapter 4 because of problems with overdispersion. The presence of overdispersion may be confirmed by examining the ratio of the deviance to the degrees of freedom[36] when a Poisson regression model is run. We examined these ratios for our data using this methodology and obtained results that were greater than 1.5 for all three Poisson regression models. Consequently, we felt that negative binomial regressions would be a more appropriate choice.

As with other multivariate regression models, the negative binomial regression model may be represented with an equation showing the constituents that determine it. This equation, however, also includes a "disturbance term, which accounts for the overdispersion." Allison (1999) describes this equation as follows:

$$\text{Log } \lambda_i = \beta 0 + \beta_1 X_{i1} + \beta_2 X_{i2} + \dots + \beta k X k_i + \sigma \varepsilon_i$$

The dependent variable. y_i, is assumed to have a "Poisson distribution with expected value λ_i conditional on ε_i," and the exp (ε_i) is assumed to have a "standard gamma distribution."[37]

The negative binomial regression produces coefficients and incidence rate ratios that can be interpreted in a somewhat similar manner to the

34.   M. K. Bulsara, C. D. J. Holman, E. A. Davis, and T. W. Jones, "Evaluating Risk Factors Associated with Severe Hypoglycaemia in Epidemiology Studies—What Method Should We Use?" *Diabetic Medicine* 21, no. 8 (August 2004): 914–19.

35.   Allison, *Logistic Regression Using the SAS System*.

36.   Ibid.

37.   Ibid.

coefficients and odds ratios produced by logistic regression. The coefficients may be exponentiated to obtain incidence rate ratios, which must be significantly different than 1.0. For example, if the incidence rate ratio is higher than 1.0, then the outcome or event occurs at a significantly higher rate when xi (exposure variable) increases by one level or unit. If the incidence rate ratio is lower than 1.0, then the event occurs at a significantly lower rate when xi increases by one level or unit. If the incidence rate ratio does not significantly differ from 1.0, then the rates of the event are essentially the same. Similar to other multivariate regressions, incidence rate ratios estimate associations with the exposure variables when controlling for other potentially confounding factors.[38]

Alternatively, the difference in rates may be explained by the percentage increases or decreases per level or unit change in the exposure variable. In Poisson regression, this percentage change may be obtained using the formula 100 $(e\beta - 1)$, as given by Allison.[39] Calhoun et al. also interpreted results for their negative binomial regressions models in this manner for their study of medical service utilization.[40]

Examples of the interpretation of the incidence rate ratios and the percentage change using our results from Chapter 4 are included here. For the negative binomial regression model examining the outcome of primary care use by all types of enrollees (see Chapter 4), females had an incidence rate ratio of 1.43 and a change of 43%. This means that females had a significantly higher rate of primary care use then men, controlling for all other factors in the model. Given the percentage change, one could say that women made 43% more primary care visits than men, controlling for all other factors in the model. For the outcome of emergency room use by all types of registrants (also in Chapter 4), the results showed an incidence rate ratio of 0.70 and a change of −30%. Thus, women had a significantly lower rate of emergency room utilization than the men, controlling for all other factors in the model, and women made 30% fewer emergency room visits than men, controlling for other factors in the model. Though the incidence rate ratio is often used to estimate the relative risk, Petrie and Sabin (2005) assert that this will be accurate only when the event is rare.[41] In this book, primary care and emergency room utilization do not constitute rare events, so the level of risk may not be accurately known.

---

38. Petrie and Sabin, *Medical Statistics at a Glance*.
39. Allison, *Logistic Regression Using the SAS System*.
40. Patrick S. Calhoun, Hayden B. Bosworth, Steven C. Grambow, Tara K. Dudley, and Jean C. Beckham, "Medical Service Utilization by Veterans Seeking Help for Posttraumatic Stress Disorder," *American Journal of Psychiatry* 159, no. 12 (December 2002): 2081–86.
41. Petrie and Sabin, *Medical Statistics at a Glance*.

In conclusion, measures of association such as the odds ratio, relative risk, or incidence rate ratio are useful tests for identifying factors that are related to a specified outcome or event. Multivariate regressions provide a convenient way of examining the strength and direction of these associations for a given exposure while controlling for other factors.

Populations Examined in Chapter 5

Source Populations for the Calculation of Utilization Rates

Chapter 5 provided an overview of VODI's Disease Management Program, along with its accomplishments and impact. In that chapter, a number of analyses were performed to determine how the Disease Management Program positively affected the health care utilization patterns of its participants. One methodological approach described there compares disease management participants and nonparticipants for the utilization rates of emergency, primary care, and inpatient/specialty care visits, as well as the total combined rates of utilization for those three categories of service.

The utilization rates reported in Chapter 5 could have been carried out with two different populations. One source population (N = 15,421) for comparing the utilization rates was made up of VODI Disease Management Program participants (N = 93) and nonparticipants (N = 1,355) in the population of all VODI patients enrolled before January 1, 2004. This included some enrollees who did not utilize any of the principal care services (primary, emergency, and inpatient/specialty care), as well as enrollees who did utilize at least one of these services. Rates were determined using this population so as to correct for the artificial inflation that may be seen when populations are restricted to those who utilized services; in this way, a comparison to national norms may be made. However, these utilization rates were also calculated for the VODI Disease Management Program participants (N = 66) and nonparticipants (N = 944) from the source population that had already been restricted to those who had utilized at least one principal care service after enrollment (N = 8,585). These rates were calculated to allow a more direct comparison of the results presented in Chapter 4, in which all of the analyses were restricted to enrollees who had utilized at least one principal service.

Table A: Utilization Rates of Care Management Participants Enrolled in2003

Utilization Rate (per 100 members)								
Care Management status	Cohort	Primary Care		Emergency Room		Inpatient/ Specialty Care		Overall	
No care management received	944	143.4	1.4	70.8	0.7	134.6	1.3	348.6	3.5
Care management received	66	280.3	2.8	74.2	0.7	128.8	1.3	483.3	4.8

Note: Both cohorts compared clients who were identified as having one or more of the four chronic conditions or a history of high emergency room utilization. Overall utilization includes primary care, emergency room, and inpatient/specialty care visits. Rates are based on service visits within one year of the registration date, excluding visits on the actual date of enrollment.

In Chapter 5, Table 5.5 compares rates of both active and inactive enrollees (the first source population described earlier) and therefore presents more conservative (lower) use rates. Those rates include people who may have left the program, as described in Chapter 3. In comparison, Table A shows utilization rates based only on active enrollees. However, a comparison of Table 5.5 and Table A shows very similar patterns when the disease management group is compared with the non–disease managed group. In both tables, the disease management group used significantly more primary care services than the non–disease management group. Both groups used approximately equal emergency room and inpatient/specialty care.

Comparison of Cohorts Based on Year of Enrollment

Another issue was examined for the disease management participant and nonparticipant cohorts drawn from the source population of active and inactive enrollees in the VODI program. This issue involves an assessment of the comparability of demographic and health care characteristics possessed by the disease management participants and non-participants enrolled only in 2003. This assessment is shown in Table 5.1 of Chapter 5, with the only difference being that those two cohorts were enrolled in both 2003 and 2004. However, the comparison of the utilization rates for the disease management participants and nonparticipants (Table 5.5) was restricted to clients enrolled before January 1, 2004, to ensure that they had at least one year of enrollment in which to utilize services. The analysis of characteristics for the two cohorts enrolled only in 2003 repeated the same statistical tests to check for significant differences between the two groups, as those shown for the 2003–2004 enrollees. These additional tests showed the same significant differences, except that the 2003 nonparticipants also showed a significantly lower percentage of enrollees enrolled through primary care sites compared to the disease management participants (X2 = 6.89, *df* =2, p-value = 0.032).

Although the results show statistical significance, comparisons may still be made if the results are interpreted conservatively. For example, though a greater percentage of disease management participants had more than one qualifying chronic condition compared to nonparticipants, this difference may be expected to increase emergency room and inpatient/specialty care utilization, thereby underestimating the impact of the Disease Management Program. Furthermore, disease management participants who had frequent emergency room use as their only eligibility criteria showed a very small sample size and, as a result, may not provide the most stable estimate for comparison of this measure. Finally, although the 2003 cohort showed more primary care enrollees, an increased amount of primary care use may still be noted in the analysis that was restricted to emergency room enrollees. Thus, the differences reported for the cohorts, regardless of whether the enrollment period was 2003 only or 2003–2004, were not great enough to prevent a valid comparison of these two groups.

Index